Statistical Concepts

Statistical Concepts
A Basic Program

Foster Lloyd Brown

State University of New York, Oneonta

Jimmy R. Amos

Eastern Idaho Community Mental Health Center

Oscar G. Mink

University of Texas

THIRD EDITION

HarperCollins*CollegePublishers*

Acquisitions Editor: Catherine Woods
Developmental Editor: Lesley Atlas
Project Coordination, Text and Cover Design: York Production Services
Electronic Production Manager: Christine Pearson
Electronic Page Makeup: York Production Services
Printer and Binder: R.R. Donnelley & Sons Company
Cover Printer: The Lehigh Press, Inc.

For permission to use copyrighted material, grateful acknowledgement is made to the copyright holders on pp. 161-174, which are hereby made part of this copyright page.

Statistical Concepts: A Basic Program

Brown, Foster Lloyd.
     Statistical concepts / Foster Brown. — 3rd ed.
         p. cm.
     Includes bibliographical references (p. 175) and index.
     ISBN 0-673-99440-6
      1. Mathematical statistics—Programmed instruction. I. Title.
QA276.B74   1995   94-35670
519.5'07'7—dc20   CIP

Dedication

I dedicate this text to my wife, Rita, who not only gave support and did word-processing, but was a sharp and valuable critic, tightening, clarifying, and softening my pedantry.

Foster Lloyd Brown

Contents

Preface to the Third Edition   xi
Tips to the Student   xiii

Descriptive Statistical Methods   1

Frequency Distribution   1
   Frequency Polygons   2
   Histograms   2
Open Book Quiz on Frequency Distribution   5

Averages   6
   The Mean: Practical Computations   7
   Skewness   8
   Median   13
   Mode   15
   Bimodality and Multimodality   17
Open Book Quiz on Averages   20

The Normal Curve   20
   Example   20
   Standard Deviation   24
   The z Score   27
   Normal Curve Areas   27
Open Book Quiz on the Normal Curve   34

Standard Scores   35
   Examples   35
   Computation   36
   A Caution   38

Variability   38
   Range   38
   Standard Deviation Revisited   39
   Computing Standard Deviations   40
   Sum of Squares (Deviation Method)   40
   Sum of Squares (Practical Computation)   42
      Inferential Statistics   45
      Population and Sample   46
      Point Estimation   48
   Computer Quick Start   52

Open Book Quiz on Variability   54

Inferential Statistical Methods *55*

Probability   *55*

The Null Hypothesis   *56*
Direct Probability   *58*
Laws of Probability   *60*

Open Book Quiz on Probability   *62*

Confidence Intervals   *62*

Standard Error of the Mean   *64*
Distribution of Means   *65*
Degrees of Freedom   *66*
Computing the Confidence Interval   *67*
Correlated *t* Test   *69*

Open Book Quiz on Confidence Interval of the Mean   *71*

Correlation Coefficient: The Ups and Downs of Relationships   *72*

Practical Computation   *76*
Interpretation of r^2 *79*
Significance of a Correlation Coefficient   *80*

Computer Quick Start   *81*

Open Book Quiz on Correlation Coefficient   *84*

Regression   *85*

Linear Equation   *85*
Symbols   *86*
Relationship to *r*   *92*
Least Squares Criterion   *93*
Predicting Behavior: Practical Computations   *101*

Computer Quick Start   *102*

Open Book Quiz on Regression   *105*

Analysis of Variance (ANOVA)   *106*

Symbols   *108*
ANOVA: Practical Computations   *112*

Computer Quick Start   *118*

Open Book Quiz on Analysis of Variance (ANOVA)   *121*

Chi-Square Frequencies: (Expected and Observed)   *122*

One-Way (One-Dimensional) Chi-Square   *122*
Two-Way (Two-Dimensional) Chi-Square   *126*
Significance Testing of Chi-Square   *130*

Computer Quick Start   *135*

Open Book Quiz on Chi-Square   *139*

Measurement   *140*

   Scores   *140*
      Raw Scores   *140*
      Ranks   *141*
      Percentile Ranks   *141*
      Percentile Scores   *144*
      Standard Scores (Revisited)   *145*
   Reliability and Validity   *146*
      Reliability   *148*
      Validity   *150*
   Standard Error of Measurement   *154*

   Open Book Quiz on Measurement   *158*

   You Can't Fool Me: Spotting Fallacies in Statistical Thought   *158*

Appendices   *161*

   A: Tables of Critical Values   *161*
      Table A Critical Values of the Correlation Coefficient   *162*
      Table B The 5 Percent Points for the Distribution of *F*   *163*
      Table C The I Percent Points for the Distribution of *F*   *164*
      Table D Distribution of *t* Probability   *165*
      Table E Distribution of Chi-Square   *166*
      Table F Areas and Ordinates of Normal Curve in Terms of *z*   *167*
   B: Bibliography   *175*

   C: Use of Computer Packages: An Overview   *176*

   D: Answers to Open Book Quizzes   *183*

   E: Evaluative Data   *188*

Index   *189*

Preface to the Third Edition

Because earlier editions of this book have been extremely successful and long lived, this third edition expands opportunities for the reader without sacrificing the brevity and clarity of the earlier editions.

This edition differs from the second principally in the following features:

1. Addition of **Computer Quick Start** sections on **Minitab, SAS,** and **SPSS.** For those who plan to include computers in the course of study, these sections allow rapid access to the power of computer packages. For others, these sections will serve as brief introductions to how computer output looks and gentle encouragement on the ease of use of Minitab, SAS, and SPSS.
2. A brief section on critical thinking to conclude the book.
3. Extensive fine tuning on sequencing of material. For example, standard scores appears early in the text with z scores, and regression analysis directly follows correlation analysis.
4. Nearly every frame has been reedited for clarity and directness.

I hope that this edition, through selection of topics, will continue to be useful as a course supplement. Used in its entirety, it should now serve as a core text for one-quarter and one-semester courses in statistical methods.

I am indebted to the Literary Executor of the late Sir Ronald A. Fisher, F.R.S., to Dr. Frank Yates, F.R.S., and to Longman Group Ltd., London, for permission to reprint Tables III, IV, and VI from their book *Statistical Tables for Biological, Agricultural and Medical Research.*

Thanks are extended to MINITAB Inc., the SAS Institute, and SPSS Inc. who let me use their latest software and documentation.

I would also like to thank the following reviewers, who provided valuable commentary:

Robert Barraclough, West Virginia University;
Mark Lewis, University of Texas at Tyler;
and Roger R. Miller, Smith College.

Foster Lloyd Brown

Tips to the Student

Some of you are reluctant to study statistics because you have heard that it is difficult and highly technical. This text was carefully designed to present the material in small steps and to check your growing understanding at each step. Even the most mathematically unskilled should understand and enjoy this book. The book is presented in a series of numbered *frames*. Each frame consists of three parts:

1. Explanation
2. Question
3. Corresponding *book response*

Respond to each frame **before** you see the *book response*.

To help you avoid seeing the book response before you respond to the frame, use a mask of paper, which you slide down the page as you progress. When you see a boldface line, stop the motion of the paper. You can thus make sure that you understand each frame as it comes along. This is especially helpful when you are tired or preoccupied. A programmed text such as this one is well adapted to study during odd free moments. If you are a busy person, you might wish to work this way, although you will achieve the best results if you give this text the same undivided attention you would give a classroom text.

Some of you will spend less than nine hours working the program. These hours will enable you to master some important concepts necessary for understanding today's research literature in the behavioral and social sciences.

Descriptive Statistical Methods

Frequency Distribution

1. Such things as **test scores, class rank, weight,** and **income** are called **variables.** Income, for instance, is called a variable because income values vary. In general, things that vary in value from case to case or from time to time are called _____.

    Variables

2. The number of times a particular value of a variable occurs is referred to as the **frequency** of that value. If 17 students receive a score of 70 on a test, then the score of 70 has a _____ of 17.

    Frequency

3. A **distribution** is a series of separate values such as scores that are arranged or ordered according to magnitude. If the scores 13, 11, 11, 9, 9, 9, 8, 5 represent performance on some test, they could be called a _____.

    Distribution

4. A set of ordered scores and their corresponding frequencies is called a frequency distribution. This can be represented in table or graph form. The table below shows the number of times a score occurs in its group. This table gives a frequency _____.

Scores	Frequency
13	I
11	II
9	III
8	I
5	I

    Distribution

Frequency Polygons

5. Frequency distributions can also be graphically illustrated. The two most common graphs that are used to illustrate frequency distributions are the **frequency polygon** and the **histogram.** If scores and their frequencies are illustrated with points connected by lines, the result is called a **frequency polygon.** Because the illustration below shows the frequency of particular grades by the height of points that are connected by lines, it is called a frequency _____.

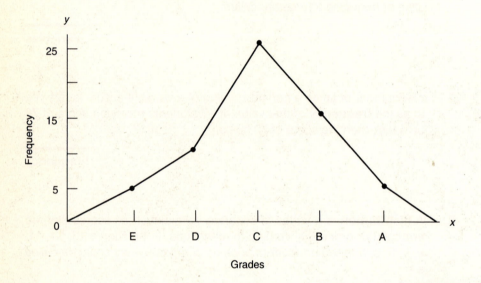

Grades

Polygon

Histograms

6. A frequency distribution may be graphed by using rectangular boxes. Such a graph is called a **histogram** or **bar graph.** The long direction of the bars, which may be vertical or horizontal, indicates the frequency. The following graphs are called _____.

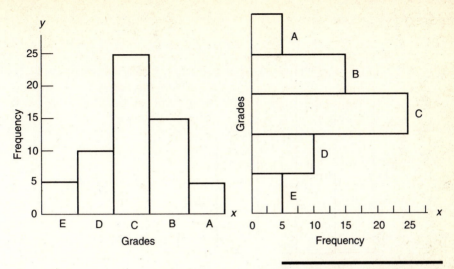

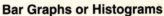

Bar Graphs or Histograms

7.   Two useful terms for thinking about graphs are *X* axis and *Y* axis.

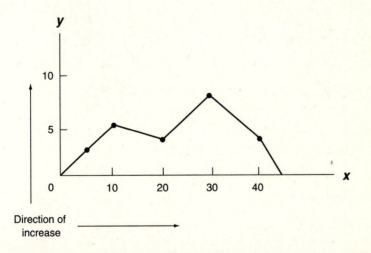

Direction of increase

The values on the *Y* axis change as we go up or down. The values on the *X* axis change as we go left or right. In the following figure the frequency is on the _____ axis.

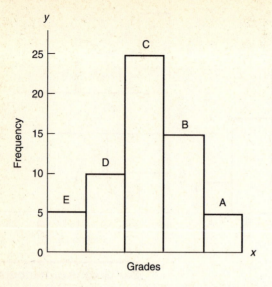

Grades

8. Here the frequency is on the _____ axis.

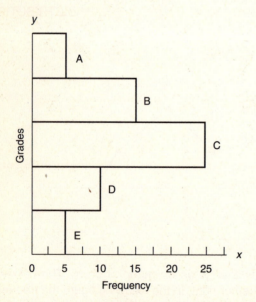

$\overline{X}$

9.   The two most common graphs that were used to illustrate frequency distributions are the frequency polygon and the _____.

Graph A is a _____. Graph B is a _____.

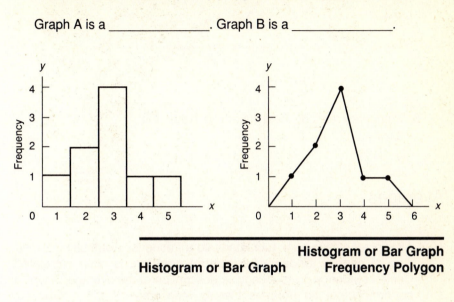

Histogram or Bar Graph

Histogram or Bar Graph   Frequency Polygon

OPEN BOOK QUIZ ON FREQUENCY DISTRIBUTION
(Answers on page 183)

1. Construct a frequency distribution to represent the following scores: 0, 1, 2, 2, 2, 2, 3, 3, 3, 5.

2. Draw a histogram to illustrate the frequency distribution in Problem 1. Use the Y axis for frequency.

3. Using a dotted line, draw a frequency polygon to represent the frequency distribution in Problem 1. Superimpose this drawing over the histogram from Problem 2.

4. For the following frequency polygon, label the X and the Y axis.

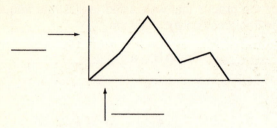

5. Frequency can be designated on either the _____ or _____ axis.

Averages

10. After scores have been tabulated into a frequency distribution, a measure of **central tendency,** or **central position,** is often calculated. Central tendency gives a concise description of the average or typical performance of the group as a whole. Measures of _____ tendency allow us to compare two or more groups in terms of typical performance.

Central

11. In statistics there are several "averages" or measures of _____ _____ in common use. Three of these are (a) the mean, (b) the median, and (c) the mode.

Central Tendency

12. The mean is generally the most familiar and most useful to us. The mean is computed by dividing the **sum of the scores** by the **total number of scores.** The formula for the mean is:

Mean = sum of the scores/_____

N or Total Number of Scores

The Mean: Practical Computations

This section on the mean is not meant to teach you how to compute a mean (which you can probably already do), but to introduce some symbols and a way of learning how to do more complex computations.

Using the notes and example problem, solve the practice problem on the right.

13. Sum the scores and label the sum as ΣX. The uppercase Greek letter sigma, Σ, may be read as "sum of." X stands for scores.

I Did This		You Try This	
	X		
Don	0	Ima	0
Ray	2	Lil	2
Jan	4	Dot	2
May	4	Hal	3
Joy	4	Sue	8
Jim	4		
Sam	6		
Fay	6		
Art	6		
$\Sigma X =$	36	$\Sigma X =$	

$\Sigma X = 15$

14. N symbolizes the number of scores.

I Did This	You Try This
$N = 9$	$N =$

5

15. The mean, symbolized by $\overline{X}$ (read "X bar") and in computer output by MEAN is ΣX divided by N.

I Did This	You Try This
$\overline{X} = \Sigma X/N$	$\overline{X} =$
$= 36/9$	
$= 4$	

3

16. Finding the arithmetic mean of a distribution is the same as finding the center of moment, or the balance point, in a solid block. If a distribution were suspended by the mean, it would hang level or balanced. The

mean, whose symbol is _____, is the center of moment in a frequency distribution.

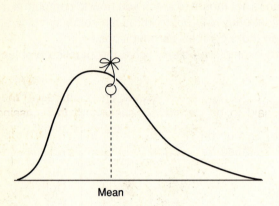

Mean

$\overline{X}$ or Mean

Skewness

17. If extremely high or extremely low scores are added to a distribution, the mean tends to shift toward those scores. If the center of gravity of the distribution is shifted to one side or the other of the curve, the curve becomes **skewed.** The following curve has a few extremely low scores. Consequently, this distribution is _____.

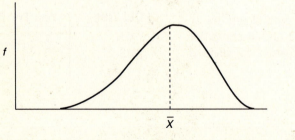

$\overline{X}$

Skewed

18. Extreme scores, either high or low, tend to _____ a distribution.

Skew

19. If a distribution is massed so that the greatest number of scores is at the right end of the curve and a few scores are scattered at the left end, the curve is said to be **negatively** skewed. If the massing of scores is at the left end of the curve with the tail extending to the right end, then the curve is **positively** skewed. Graph A illustrates _____ skewness. Graph B illustrates _____ skewness.

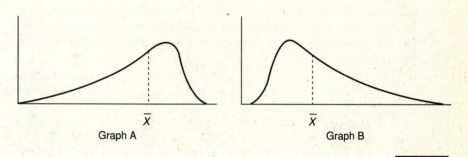

Graph A   Graph B

Negative
Positive

20. If a quiz were very easy for a group, so that there were many high scores and a scattering of a few low scores—for example, 2, 6, 7, 8, 8, 8, 9, 9, 9, 9, 10—it would be _____ _____.

Negatively Skewed

21. The following graph's tail is extending to the right because of a few extremely high scores. It is therefore _____ skewed.

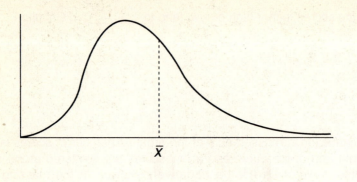

Positively

22. A curve is **symmetrical** when one half of the curve is a mirror image of the other half. If you folded a frequency polygon at the mean and the two halves were the same, then the frequency distribution represented by the polygon would be _____.

Symmetrical

23. If we added extreme scores to one end of a previously symmetrical curve, the mean would shift toward those extreme scores. Would the curve then be symmetrical or not symmetrical? _____

Not Symmetrical (or Asymmetrical)

24. Regardless of whether the curve is symmetrical or asymmetrical, the mean is always the center of balance. Does this mean that the mean is always centrally located in asymmetrical curves? _____

No

25. Let's illustrate this point by placing a distribution along the interval scale shown below. Each figure represents one person. The scale

would obviously balance if a fulcrum were under the middle number, 4. To verify this, calculate the mean. _____ Is this distribution symmetrical? _____

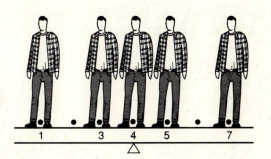

Mean = 20/5 = 4
Yes

26. If the person with a score of 7 had scored 12, what would be the mean? _____ Place a fulcrum (Δ) at the balance point of the scale below at number _____. Is the fulcrum centrally located? _____ Is this distribution symmetrical? _____

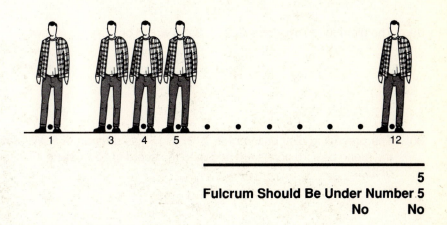

5
Fulcrum Should Be Under Number 5
No   No

27. What would be the mean for the above distribution if the person who scored 12 had instead scored 22? _____

28.   When a curve is positively skewed (see Graph A), the mean is located to the _____ (right or left) of most of the cases. When a curve is neg-atively skewed (see Graph B) the mean is located to the _____ of the cases. Each dot is one case.

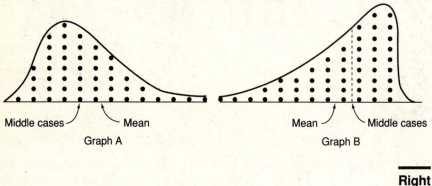

Middle cases ↗   ↖ Mean   Mean ↗   ↖ Middle cases

Graph A   Graph B

———
Right
Left

29.   The distribution of scores 2, 2, 3, 3, 15 would be _____ skewed.

———
Positively

30.   The preceding distribution of 2, 2, 3, 3, 15 has a mean of 5. What will the mean be if 10 points are added to the score of 15 (making it a score of 25)? _____

31.   We see that by adding 10 points to the score of 15, the mean of the distribution 2, 2, 3, 3, 15 is raised by two points because the mean is an arithmetic average and each score contributes to its value. When 10 is added, it is averaged or distributed equally among the five scores.

This has the same effect as adding a constant of two points to each score (10 points/5 scores = 2 points per score). When two points are added to each score, the mean is raised by _____ points.

—
2

32. When a constant is added to each score of a distribution, that constant is added to the previous mean to find the new mean. If each score of a distribution is multiplied by a constant, the new mean is found by multiplying the old mean by that _____.

—————
Constant

33. The distribution 0, 2, 2, 3, 13 has a mean of 4. What would the mean be if each score were increased by 2? _____ What would the mean be if each score were multiplied by 2? _____

—
6
8

Median

34. When an extreme score is added to a distribution, the mean no longer represents a centrally located score but a measure that is more typical of the extreme score. This causes us to rely on another measure of central tendency, which is called the **median,** or the middle score. The median is abbreviated **Md** or **Mdn.** The measure of central tendency that is less affected by the addition of an extreme score is the

_____.

—————
Median

35. The median is a **point** on a scale of measurement above which are half the cases and below which are the other half of the cases. Note that the median is defined as a point and not as a specific measurement, for example, a score or a case. From the distribution 4, 6, 8, 10,

12, it is easy to see that 8 is the middle score. The score of 8 is at the **point** where there are two scores above and two scores below; hence 8 is the median. What is the median of 11, 11, 14, 19, 19? _____

14

36. To obtain the median, the measures are arranged in ascending order from the lowest to the highest measure. Then by counting up this scale, the point is selected above and below which there are equal numbers of cases. The value of this point is the middle or the _____ case.

Median

37. The median of the distribution 3, 2, 0, 1, 6 is found by first arranging the measures from the lowest to the _____ number (0, 1, 2, 3, 6). Then we find the middle score or case, which is _____.

Highest
2

38. When there is an even number of cases, average the two middle scores. The median of 0, 6, 9, and 12 is _____.

7.5

39. When a distribution has a midpoint score with a frequency greater than 1 (e.g., 5, 6, 9, 9, 9, 11), use the midpoint score as the median just as before (the median is thus 9 for this case). There is a more exact solution, but it is seldom used, and the exact answer, when rounded to the nearest whole number, is always the same as that obtained by the method given here. The median of the distribution 0, 2, 4, 4, 4, 4, 6, 6, 6 is _____.

4

40. The usefulness of the median as an indicator of central tendency is increased when the end score is extreme. For example, the median of 0, 6, 9, 10, 10 is _____. The mean of this distribution is 7 (i.e., 35/5). If the extreme number 55 is substituted for one of the 10s, giving the distribution 0, 6, 9, 10, 55, the median remains _____, but the mean is now _____.

9
9
16

Mode

41. A third measure of central tendency is the mode. It may be defined as the one value or score that occurs with the most frequency. The mode of the series 2, 3, 4, 4, 4, 5, 5 is 4. The mode of the series 7, 8, 10, 10, 10, 11, 11 is _____. The median is _____.

10   10

42. Is it possible for a distribution to have a median and a mode that have the same value? _____

Yes

43. The mode is used as a simple, "eyeball" average to show quickly the center of concentration of a frequency distribution. What is the mode, or the rough average, of the following frequency distribution? _____

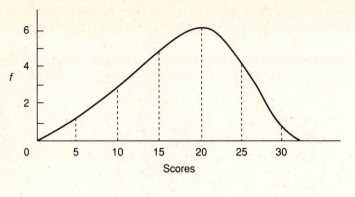

Scores

20

44. When *N* is small, the mode can be deceptive. The frequency polygon shown below is an extreme example. It is clear that the mode is 10, but it does not give a good idea of the average case. The mean is 25 ($\Sigma X/N$ = 125/5). The cases, in ascending order, are 10, 10, 25, 35, 45, so the median is _____.

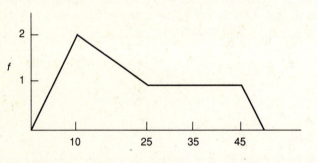

25

45. The mode is used, in preference to either the median or the mean, when a measure of the **most characteristic** value of a group is desired. What is meant by the most characteristic value can be exemplified by clothing fashions. The _____ is what is being worn the most.

Mode

46. The mode is also used to be sure that the average that you get really exists. In finding the average size of automobile tires that are bought, the mean size might be a tire that does not exist. Therefore, one would want to know the size of tire that is bought most often. This would be the _____.

Mode

Bimodality and Multimodality

47. In addition to serving as a measure of central tendency, the concept of modality is useful in describing the shape of some distributions. If a histogram or a frequency distribution has two peaks, it is referred to as a **bimodal** distribution. If a distribution has more than two peaks, it is called **multimodal.** The following histogram appears to have two separate concentrations of frequencies, so it can be described as _____.

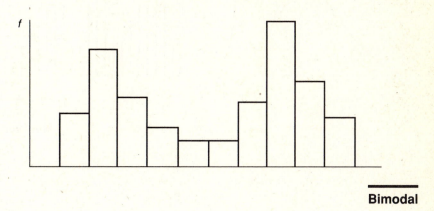

Bimodal

48. When a distribution is bimodal, it quietly whispers to us that the variable being measured may have two very different groups. If we were to measure people's ability to lift a dead weight from the floor to straight

overhead, a sample might show a bimodal distribution. What underlying variable might cause this? _____

Gender (Male or Female) or Perhaps Those Who Lift Weights and Those Who Don't.

49. For a distribution to be described as bimodal or multimodal, the peaks don't necessarily have to be exactly the same. It's the general shape that counts. The shape of the frequency distribution illustrated below by the frequency polygon is _____. The distribution of the histogram is _____.

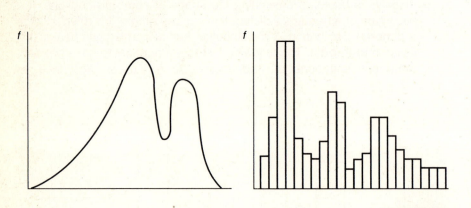

Bimodal
Multimodal

50. The score that occurs with the most frequency is the mode; hence the mode is not influenced by extreme scores. The mean is greatly influenced by extreme scores. On the basis of these two statements and the preceding exercises on the median, it is evident that line A indicates the mode, since it is not influenced by the extreme scores. Line B

is not affected as much as line C; thus it must be the _____. Line C is the _____; it is influenced the most by the extreme scores.

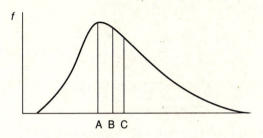

Median
Mean

51. The frequency distribution below is _____ skewed. Line A indicates the _____. Line B indicates the _____. Line C indicates the _____. The mean of a negatively skewed distribution is located to the left of the mode. The mean of a positively skewed distribution is located to the _____ of the mode.

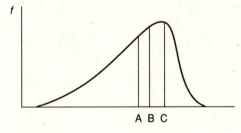

	Negatively
Mean	**Median**
	Mode
	Right

OPEN BOOK QUIZ ON AVERAGES
(Answers on page 183)

1. For the distribution 8, 5, 6, 9, 3, 5, compute the:
   a. Mean _____
   b. Median _____
   c. Mode _____

2. How would you describe the shape of the distribution 2, 2, 3, 3, 3, 3, 4, 4, 5, 6, 12, 19? _____   _____

3. If a small company had mostly low-paid employees but one very highly paid employee, what would be the most appropriate measure of central tendency to indicate the salary level of that company?

The Normal Curve

Example

52. Suppose that we persuaded 1000 kangaroos to line up behind signs according to their weights. The signs run from left to right in order of increasing weight from 95 pounds to 164 pounds. The number of kangaroos in any one line is the frequency of that weight. The number of 130 pounders is the _____ of 130 pounders.

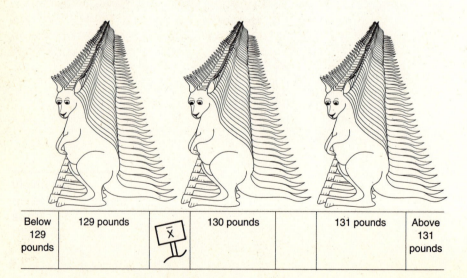

Below 129 pounds	129 pounds	$\bar{x}$	130 pounds		131 pounds	Above 131 pounds

Frequency

53. From an airplane the place where this event was occurring might look like the diagram below. Each dot represents a _____.

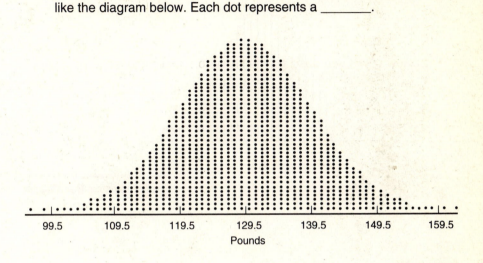

99.5   109.5   119.5   129.5   139.5   149.5   159.5

Pounds

Kangaroo

54. Assuming that the kangaroos are separated from each other by the same amount of space, the **relative area could be estimated by using the proportion of kangaroos (dots) in some interval.** For example, with 1000 cases the 50 heaviest kangaroos would occupy the extreme right 5 percent of the crowd. The 25 lightest kangaroos would occupy the extreme left _____ percent of the crowd.

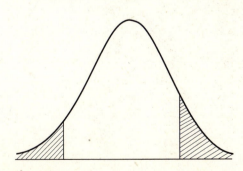

2.5

55. If each column of kangaroos is represented by a rectangular box, **we** have our old friend the _____

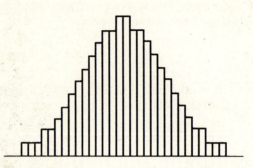

Histogram or Bar Graph

56. If we have a very large number of subjects and use very small **weight** categories, the irregular steplike curve will become continuous. In this case the resulting figure approaches a special type of curve called the **normal** or **bell curve.** In frequency distributions, normality is not associated with small groups of subjects but rather with very _____ numbers of subjects.

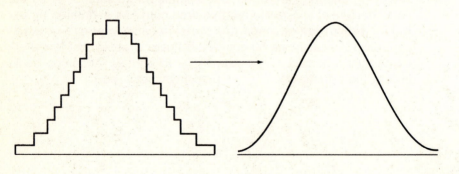

Large

57. Normal, as used here, means ordinary or common. Other distributions are not abnormal. Another name for this rather common or normal distribution is the bell curve. Two names that might apply to a distribution that is symmetrical, is high in the center, and has long tails on each side are _____ and _____.

Normal   Bell

58. Quantitative data gathered about a variety of natural phenomena, including many mental and social traits, form distributions that, though not precisely normal in distribution, may be closely described by the normal _____.

Curve or Distribution

59. The distributions of such diverse properties as achievement test scores, IQ, and height and weight of people form approximately _____.

Normal Curves or Normal Distributions

60. Although the thin tails of the mathematical normal curve get closer and closer to the baseline, they never touch it. With actual data there is ultimately a heaviest person, a shortest person, a highest score, and so on, and the curve touches the baseline. What would be the frequency of a weight so high that nobody was that heavy? _____

Zero

61. The bell-shaped curve illustrated in Frame 53 approximates a **normal curve.** Note the following properties:

   a. It is symmetrical.
   b. The mean, median, and mode have the same value (in this instance, 129.5).

c. Thus there are equal numbers of scores on either side of the mean.

What proportion of cases for this sample of kangaroos exceed the mean of 129.5? _____
What percent? _____

One Half or .50
50 Percent

62. There are two points on the symmetrical normal curve where the curve changes direction from convex to concave. These points are **points of inflection** (see Graph A). Are the inflection points on Graph B at lines W, lines X, or lines Y? _____

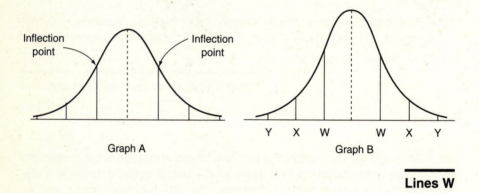

Graph A   Graph B

Lines W

Standard Deviation

63. Perpendicular lines drawn from the points of inflection to the *X* axis may be regarded as marking off one unit of distance or deviation from the mean (or central axis). If we use this distance as a standard, a uniform method of dividing the baseline into equal segments (**standard deviations**) can be established. If the central axis is designated as zero, the line that is one standard deviation to the right would be plus one (+1), and the line that is one standard deviation to the left would be _____.

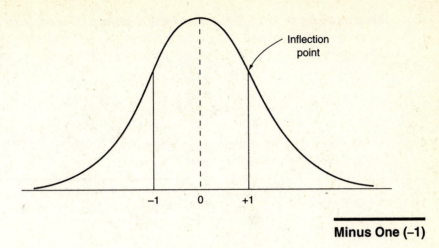

Minus One (–1)

64. Mathematically, the points −1 and +1 are situated one unit of distance or standard deviation from the mean. These two points are designated as ±1 (read as "plus and/or minus one"). Two units of distance or deviation from the mean are labeled as +2 and _____.

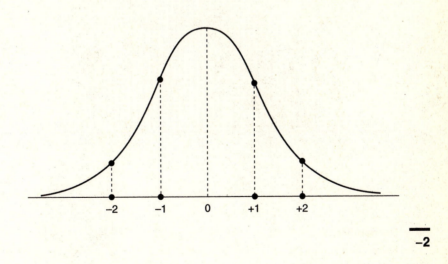

–2

65. Let's examine again the weight distribution of kangaroos. We will treat the mean as being 129.5 pounds. Note that the inflection points are about 10 pounds on either side of the mean. We will treat the inflection

points as being at 119.5 pounds and 139.5 pounds. The distance, in pounds, from the mean to an inflection point is _____ pounds.

10

66. Ten pounds is thus the **standard deviation**. What weight would be two standard deviations above the mean? _____

129.5 + (2 ∗ 10) = 149.5 Pounds

67. For this sample of kangaroos, how many kangaroos are heavier than 149.5 pounds? (Hint: Count the dots.) _____

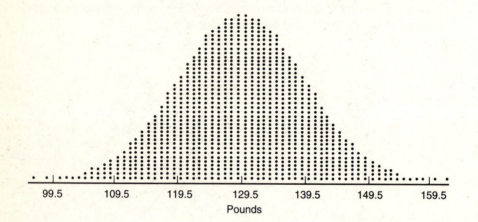

23

68. What proportion of the total would that be? _____ What percent? _____

23/1000 = .023
100 ∗ .023 = 2.3 Percent

The z Score

69. The number of standard deviations that a score is above or below the mean is called the *z* score of that score. If the score is above the mean, the *z* score is plus; if the score is below the mean, the *z* score is minus. If a score were 100 and the standard deviation were 16, a raw score of 116 would be _____ standard deviation(s) _____ the mean and would have a *z* score of _____. What is the *z* score for a score of 140? _____

One   Above
+1
+2.5

70. The *z* score can be conveniently computed by dividing a score's deviation from the mean by the standard deviation.

$$z = \frac{X - \bar{X}}{\text{standard deviation}}$$

If the mean of a distribution is 70 and the standard deviation is 6, what *z* score is assigned to a person who obtains a score of 82? _____

z = (82 − 70)/6 = 12/6 = 2

Normal Curve Areas

71. The total area under the normal curve may be set to 1. Between the mean and +1 standard deviation to the right of the mean is .3413 of the total area. Thus the area from the mean to +1 standard deviation contains 34.13 percent of the total cases. Since −1 unit of deviation is equal in area to +1 unit of deviation, _____ percent of the total cases lie in the area between a *z* score of −1 and the mean.

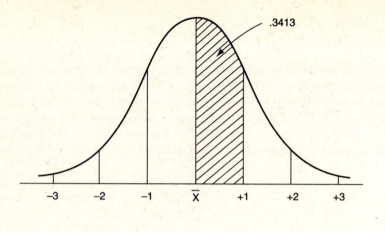

.3413

34.13

72. The symmetry and massing of normally distributed scores around the mean group is about 68.26 percent (2 ∗ 34.13) of the scores between z scores of −1 and +1. If a normal distribution has a total frequency of 1000 scores, approximately 341 scores (34.13 percent of 1000) are located between the mean and a z score of −1. In this sample, approximately 341 scores are located between the mean and +1. About how many scores are located between z scores of −1 and +1? _____

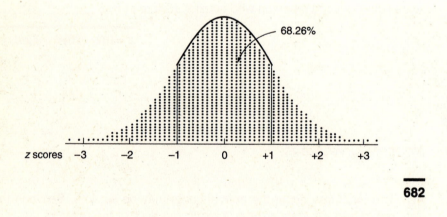

68.26%

682

73. In this frequency distribution of normally distributed scores, z scores of −1 and +1 mark off the middle _____ percent of the total scores.

They occur at the raw scores of 40 and _____.

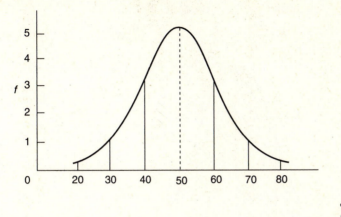

68.26 (or 68)
60

74. Although the normal curve extends infinitely to the left and to the right, the endpoints of the curve approach the baseline so closely that over 95.44 percent (see graph below) of the area or frequencies are included between the limits −2 and +2 and 99.74 percent of the cases are included between the limits −_____ and +_____.

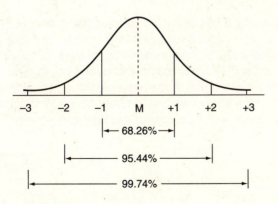

3   3

75. The percentage of cases contained between the mean of a normal curve and a *z* score of +3 is 49.87 percent (one half of 99.74 percent). The percentage of cases between the mean of a normal curve and a *z* score of −2 is about _____ percent.

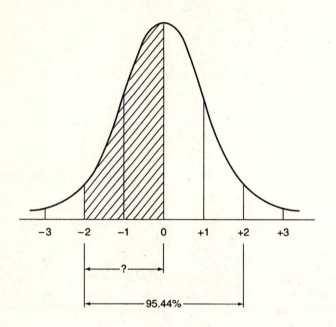

47.72

76. For practical purposes the limits of the frequencies of the normal curve rarely exceed ±3 standard deviations from the mean. The approximately twenty-six hundredths of 1 percent (.0026) of the total cases occurring outside the limits of ±3 is so slight that everybody is generally assumed to be within these limits. Approximately thirteen hundredths of 1 percent (.0013) of the total cases extend beyond +3, and approximately _____ hundredths of 1 percent of the total cases extend below −3.

Thirteen

77. Rounded to the nearest percent (note the following graph), the percentages of cases from the mean to +1, +2, and +3 are 34 percent,

48 percent, and 50 percent, respectively. The percentages of cases from the mean to −1, −2, and −3 standard deviations of a normal distribution are _____ percent, _____ percent, and _____ percent, respectively.

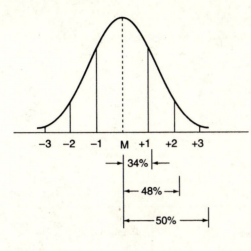

34   48   50

78. The percentage of cases below the mean is _____ percent.

50

79. The percentage of cases between the mean and +1 is about _____ percent of the total cases.

34

80. When rounded values are used, the percentage of cases below a *z* score of +1 is 84 percent (50 percent plus 34 percent) of the total cases, and the percentage of cases above +1 is _____ percent of the total cases. The percentage of cases below −1 is _____ percent.

16 (100 Minus 84)
16 (50 Minus 34)

81. People do not usually memorize the proportions above or below particular z scores but use tables such as Table 1.

Table 1   Normal Distribution
(For more complete table, see Table F in Appendix A, page 167)

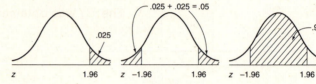

z Score	Proportion	Proportion	Proportion
0.0	.5	1.0	0.0
0.674	.25	.5	.5
1.0	.1587	.3173	.6827
1.282	.1	.2	.8
1.645	.05	.1	.9
1.960	.025	.05	.95
2.0	.0228	.0455	.9545
2.326	.01	.02	.98
2.576	.005	.01	.99
2.807	.0025	.005	.995
3.0	.00135	.0270	.99730
3.090	.001	.002	.998
3.291	.0005	.001	.999
3.719	.0001	.0002	.9998
3.891	.00005	.0001	.9999
4.0	.0000317	.0000634	.9999366
4.265	.00001	.00002	.99998
4.417	.000005	.00001	.99999
5.0	.00000029	.00000057	.99999943

82. About what proportion of normally distributed scores would have a z score equaling or exceeding 1.645? _____

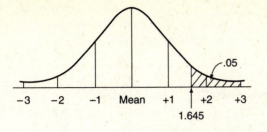

.05
The .05 was obtained by going down
the column marked z score to the desired
z (1.645). Since we want the proportion
above the z, we then go to the first
column, finding .05 or 5 percent.

83. In relation to the scores on the graph below, about what percentage of
normally distributed cases lie below 43? _____ Between 43 and 57?
_____ Below 57? _____ Above 50? _____ Below 36? _____
Total below 36 and above 50? _____

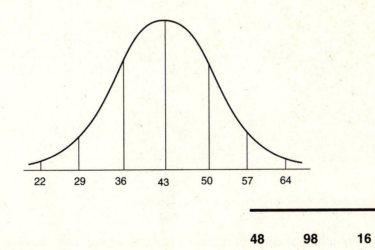

                                                                    50
                          48   **98**   **16**   **16**
                                                                    32

OPEN BOOK QUIZ ON THE NORMAL CURVE
(Answers on page 184)

1. The dots below approximate a _____ distribution.

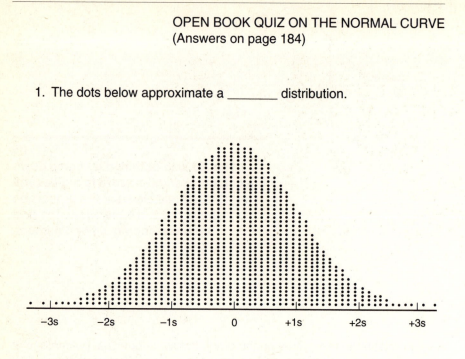

2. The scores below a z of -1.96 and above a z of $+1.96$ would make up what proportion of normally distributed scores? _____

3. What proportion of normally distributed scores would be between z scores of -1.645 and $+1.645$? _____

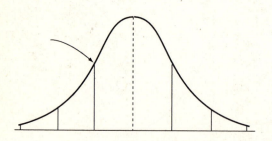

4. Label the indicated place on a normal curve. _____ _____

5. Without using a table, about what percent of normally distributed cases are within one standard deviation of the mean? _____

Standard Scores

84. Recall from earlier material that z is expressed in units of the standard deviation. It tells us **how many standard deviations a score is above or below the mean.** A score that is two standard deviations above the mean would have a z score of $+2$; a score that is one standard deviation below the mean would have a z score of _____.

___

-1

85. The mean raw score has a z score of _____ and (assuming a symmetrical distribution) would have _____ percent of the cases lying below it.

___

0.0 (or Zero)

50

86. While z scores are fine, they do have two awkward characteristics: the plus or minus sign and decimal points. To simplify: Multiply the z score by some convenient constant (thus eliminating the need for decimal points), and then add some constant that makes all of the scores positive. For example, if a z score of -2.00 were multiplied by 100, we would have _____. If 500 were added to this, the new score would be _____.

___

-200

-200 + 500 = 300

Examples

87. The mean for College Board (CEEB) scores (SAT) was arbitrarily set at 500 and the standard deviation at 100. An SAT score of 400 would indicate that a person was one standard deviation below the mean (see the figure in Frame 91). An SAT score of 700 would indicate that a person had a raw score that was _____ standard deviations _____ the mean.

___

2 Above

Computation

88. One application of the standard deviation exists in the modern form of **Stanford-Binet IQ** scores, which have a mean of 100 and a standard deviation of 16. A person who was one standard deviation above his or her age group on the raw test score would be assigned an IQ score of 116 [from 100 + 16], two standard deviations above would give an IQ score of 132 [100 + (2 * 16)], one half standard deviation below the mean would yield an IQ score of 92 [100 + (−.5 * 16)], and so on. **Wechsler IQ** scores have a mean of 100 and standard deviation of 15. What Wechsler IQ score would be equivalent to a z score of −2?

_____

---

100 + (− 2 * 15) = 100 − 30 = 70

89. It is just as easy to convert an IQ score to a z score:

$$z = \frac{X - \overline{X}}{}.$$

The Stanford Binet has a MEAN of 100 and s of 16. To convert a Stanford Binet of 116 to z, use

$$z = \frac{116 - 100}{16} = \frac{16}{16} = +1.0 .$$

The Wechsler has a MEAN of 100 and s of 15. Give z for a Wechsler score of 70. _____ How many s above her age group is a person with a Stanford Binet of 140? _____

(70 − 100)/15 = −30/15 = −2
(140 − 100)/16 = 40/16 = +2.5 or 2.5s above her age group

90. Convert each of the following *z* scores into a standard score with a mean of 500 and a standard deviation of 100.

z Score	Standard Score
−3	200
−1	_____
0	_____
+.5	_____

400
500
550

91. The figure below shows the distributions of some common standard scores.

Standard deviations from mean							
	−3s	−2s	−1s	0	+1s	+2s	+3s

Percentile ranks

1   5   10 20 30 40 50 60 70 80   90 95   99

Standard scores z scores	−3	−2	−1	0	+1	+2	+3
T scores and PSAT scores	20	30	40	50	60	70	80
CEEB (SAT) scores	200	300	400	500	600	700	800
Stanford Binet IQ	52	68	84	100	116	132	148
Wechsler IQ	55	70	85	100	115	130	145

Since the middle column of numbers gives the mean and the column to the right of it is one standard deviation above the mean, their difference is the _____ _____ for that standard score. For example, the mean of PSAT scores is 50 and one standard deviation up is 60. What is the standard deviation of PSAT scores? _____

Standard Deviation
10

A Caution

92. Each type of standard score is in reference to the individuals who took that particular test, so one type of score cannot be compared directly to another. For example, an IQ score gives one's standing compared with the entire population, whereas an SAT score gives one's standing compared only with those who took the SAT test. Is a person with a z score of 1.5 on the SAT less bright than a person with a z score of 2.0 on the Stanford Binet IQ Test? _____

Not necessarily, since the SAT test may be given to a more select group of people.

Variability

93. We have discussed descriptions of groups by frequency distributions, central tendency, and normality. Another way of describing a group is to have some index of how much variability exists. Consider the height of the two groups of people below. Both groups have a mean and median of six feet, but the more variable group is Group _____.

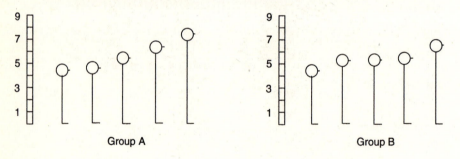

Group A   Group B

A

Range

94. One common measure of variability is the **range.** The range of a set of scores is the distance between the midpoints of the lowest and highest scores. To find the range, subtract the lowest score from the highest

score. The range of Group A with heights of 4.5, 5, 6, 7, 7.5 is 7.5 minus 4.5, or 3. The range for the less variable Group B with heights of 5, 6, 6, 6, 7 is _____.

2 (or 7 Minus 5)

95. A serious problem with the range is its vulnerability to being radically changed by one extreme score. There might be 100 children with scores going from 98 to 105. The range would be _____. Now add one child with a score of 80 to the group. The range would now be

_____.

105 – 98 = 7
105 – 80 = 25

Standard Deviation Revisited

96. The standard deviation, discussed earlier, is the other major index of variability. In the diagram below, 29 differs from 43 by two _____

_____.

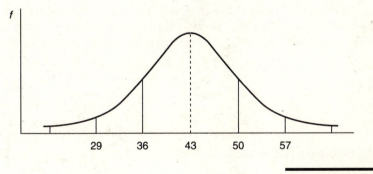

Standard Deviations

97. Suppose the following normal curves, in which the vertical deviation lines are one standard deviation apart, represent large populations. Which curve represents the more variable group? _____

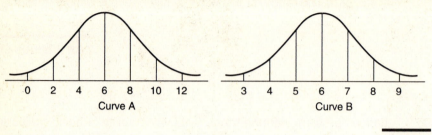

Curve A   Curve B

Curve A

98. When members of a group do not deviate much from each other, the standard deviation is small. The reverse is true for highly variable groups. Consequently, the variability or diversity of two groups can be compared by the relative size of their _____ _____.

Standard Deviations

Computing Standard Deviations

99. To compute a standard deviation from raw data, we first compute a value called the **Sum of Squares** (or simply the **SS**). We will learn two ways to do this. The first (the deviation method) is the simplest but has some practical problems; the second method looks more complicated but is easier with real data. The abbreviation for the sum of squares is _____.

SS

Sum of Squares (Deviation Method)

100. To calculate a sum of squares, the deviations from the mean are squared and then added together. To square a number, you multiply it by itself. For example, 5 squared, or $5^2 = 5 * 5 = 25$. A negative value times a negative value gives a positive value; therefore $-4^2 = -4 * -4 = 16$ $-7^2 = $ _____.

49

101. The formula for the sum of squares using the deviation method can be executed in four steps:

a. Compute the mean:

$$\overline{X}$$

b. Subtract the mean from each score to find the deviation from the mean:

$$X - \overline{X}$$

c. Square each deviation from the mean:

$$(X - \overline{X})^2$$

d. **Sum** up the **squares** of the deviations:

$$SS = \Sigma(X - \overline{X})^2$$

This is called the sum of squares (SS). It is a common mistake to use SS for the sum of all the squared scores. The SS is the sum of the squared

_____.

We will use MEAN (which is how it is expressed in computer output) and an X with a bar over it $\overline{X}$ interchangeably.

Deviations

102. Let's follow these steps with the distribution: 0, 2, 7. Calculate SS.

X	0	2	7
$\overline{X}$	___		
$X - \overline{X}$	$(0 - 3)$	$(2 - 3)$	$(\_\_\_ - \_\_\_)$
	-3	-1	___
$(X - \overline{X})^2$	9	1	___
$SS = \Sigma(X - \overline{X})^2$			___

3
7 − 3
4
16
26

Sum of Squares (Practical Computation)

The deviation method involves two passes with a calculator or computer: the first to determine the mean, the second to compute and square differences and sum those squares. It is awkward, especially if there are decimal points and negative deviations. Fortunately, there is an equivalent formula that, although it appears less friendly at first, is faster and more convenient in practice. This formula for the *SS* is (explanation will follow):

$$SS = \Sigma X^2 - \frac{(\Sigma X)^2}{N}$$

103. Two strategies for avoiding the most common errors in using this formula are the following:

   a. Make sure you do the division on the right and **then** subtract the result. A **common student error** is to do $\Sigma X^2 - (\Sigma X)^2$ and then divide by *N*.

   b. Don't confuse ΣX^2 with $(\Sigma X)^2$. For the first, we square and then sum; for the second, we sum and then square. For example, with the numbers 1 and 2, $1^2 + 2^2 = 1 + 4 = 5$, but $(1 + 2)^2 = $ _____ .

$\overline{}$
9

104. Compute ΣX as for the mean, but in addition, first square each score and sum the squares—i.e., ΣX^2

	I Did This		You Try This	
	X	X²	X	X²
Don	0	0	Ima 0	_____
Ray	2	4	Lil 2	_____
Jan	4	16	Dot 2	_____
May	4	16	Hal 3	_____
Joy	4	16	Sue 8	_____
Jim	4	16		
Sam	6	64	$\Sigma X = $ _____	
Fay	6	36	$\Sigma X^2 = $ _____	
Art	6	36		
$\Sigma X = 36$				
$\Sigma X^2 = 176$				

0
4
4
9
64
15
83

105. Square the ΣX. Note that $(\Sigma X)^2$ is the symbol. Do not confuse this with ΣX^2. For ΣX^2, we square first and then sum; for $(\Sigma X)^2$, we sum first and then square.

I Did This	You Try This
$(\Sigma X)^2 = 36^2$ $= 1296$	$(\Sigma X)^2 = ($_____$)^2$ $= $_____

15
225

106. Divide $(\Sigma X)^2$ by N. The result is called the **correction factor (CF)**.

I Did This	You Try This
$CF = (\Sigma X)^2/N$ $= 36^2/9$ $= 1296/9$ $= 144$	$CF = $_____/_____ $= $_____

225/5
45

107. Subtract CF from ΣX^2. The result is the corrected sum of squares (SS).

I Did This	You Try This
$SS = \Sigma X^2 - CF$ $= 176 - 144$ $= 32$	$SS = $_____ $- $_____ $= $_____

81 − 45
36

108. The "correction" that the *CF* makes is to compensate for using raw scores (*X*) rather than deviation scores (i.e., $X - \overline{X}$). When deviation scores are used, since their mean and sum would equal 0.0, the CF drops out. Assuming the mean of some raw scores is not zero, is the sum of the squares of the raw scores, the ΣX^2, greater than or less than the SS? _____

Greater Than

109. Subtracting a constant from, or adding a constant to, all the raw scores of a distribution does not change the value of SS. If the SS of 50, 52, 52, 58 is 36, the SS of 50 − 50, 52 − 50, 52 − 50, or 0, 2, 2, 8, is

_____.

36

110. Suppose that a population of scores is distributed so that the mean is 40 and the distance of 12 points is 1*s* (read as "one standard deviation"). Students who are one standard deviation above the mean have raw scores of _____.

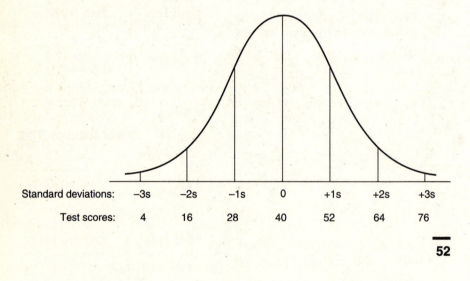

Standard deviations:	−3s	−2s	−1s	0	+1s	+2s	+3s
Test scores:	4	16	28	40	52	64	76

52

111. What is the difference, in raw score points, between the *z* scores of +1.0 and −2.0 in the above illustration? _____

36 (3 ∗ 12)

112. Compute the *SS* for 1, 3, 4, 5, 7. _____

20

113. Compute the *SS* for 0, 3, 4. _____

8.667

114. With the *SS* computed (one way or the other), it is easy to calculate the standard deviation. Simply divide the *SS* by either *N* (the number of scores) or *N* − 1 (the number of scores −1) and take the square root. To know when to divide by *N* or by *N* − 1, we need to take a brief detour into *inferential statistics.* The immediate challenge is to know when to divide the *SS* by _____ or _____.

N   N − 1

Inferential Statistics

115. The statistical ideas presented so far are useful for **describing** central tendencies, degree of variability, and relative standing with available data. These are, for the most part, **descriptive** uses of statistics. That branch of statistics is called _____ statistics.

Descriptive

116. It is frequently useful to be able to predict the future or learn things about unseen people. The branch of statistics that allows us to do this goes **beyond description** and **infers** unknown data from known data. Because it is inferential rather than descriptive, it is called _____ _____.

Inferential Statistics

Population and Sample

117. A **population,** as used in inferential statistics, is **all** of something about which an inference is to be made. It might be all the senior high school students in the United States, all the wheat in a ship's hold, all high school seniors who have IQs of 128, and English grades of A and who are female, and so on. A **sample** is a **portion** of some **population,** such as some of the seniors at Centerville High, a bucket of wheat from a ship's hold, and so on. It should be much easier to gather data about a _____ than about a _____.

Sample   Population

118. What is called a population depends upon the researcher's objectives. If the researcher wishes to infer something about the students of Centerville High, the school becomes the population and Mr. Smith's class might be the sample. If we wished to infer something about a bucket of wheat, 100 grains might be the sample and the bucket would be the _____.

Population

119. If the freshman class at a university were measured on the basis of some variable, the freshmen might be considered by a researcher as a sample of:

a. all freshmen ever to attend that university;
b. present freshmen at all universities;
c. men and women around the age of 18, and so on.

In general, the students may be considered as a _____ of various _____.

Sample
Populations

120. The terms **sample** and **population** are often used by statisticians to refer not to people or things, but to data. In this sense the sample would not be the freshman class at a university but perhaps the SAT scores of these freshmen. The population might be the SAT _____ of all freshmen ever to attend that university.

Scores

121. In the same sense a single test score by a student could be viewed as a sample of all her scores if she were to take the same test an infinite number of times (each time knowing only what she knew the first time she took the test). This hypothetical infinite set of scores would comprise the _____.

Population

122. The easiest type of sample to understand is the **simple random sample.** (There are other types of valid random samples besides the simple variety, but a complete listing would go beyond the scope of this brief discussion.) For a sample to be a simple random sample, it must be true that any single observation or score in the population has the **same chance** as any other single observation or score (of that population) of being included in the sample, and the observations must be independent of each other. Would the heights of all the freshmen at a university in one year be a simple random sample of the heights of all freshmen ever to attend that university? _____

Probably Not

123. No matter how sophisticated the statistical techniques used, we would be inviting gross error if we assumed test results to be valid for a population of all who attempt suicide when our sample consisted only of those who were unsuccessful. Such a sample is called a **biased sample.** To be representative of an entire population, a sample must **not be** _____ in regard to that population.

Biased

124. If one tried to predict the results of a presidential election by picking names from country club member lists and questioning the people selected, one would be working with a _____ sample of the U.S. population.

Biased

125. A value for a sample, such as a mean or a standard deviation, is called a **statistic.** The corresponding value for a population, such as a mean or a standard deviation, is called a **parameter.** In inferential statistics we use statistics to estimate _____.

Parameters

Point Estimation

126. Three general kinds of inferences are commonly drawn about parameters: **point estimates, confidence intervals,** and **significance tests.** In point estimation we seek the best single value that can be used to estimate a parameter. The best estimate of the mean or median of a population is the mean or median of the sample. If a sample had a mean of 120, the best estimate of the population mean would be _____. An estimate of a population mean or median based on the sample's mean or median is a point _____.

120
Estimate

127. Now back to computing standard deviations: The opposite of squaring a number is taking a square root.

$$\sqrt{25} = 5, \sqrt{16} = \underline{\hspace{1.5cm}}.$$

128. When some arithmetic occurs inside a square root sign, work the arithmetic before taking the square root.

$$\sqrt{\frac{36}{4}} = \underline{\hspace{1.5cm}}.$$

$$\overline{\sqrt{9} = 3}$$

129. The range is easier to understand and easier to calculate than the standard deviation, but it has the serious disadvantages, instability, and lack of versatility. The standard deviation (and its square, the variance) is used in many kinds of statistical analysis. Of the two (range and standard deviation), the measure of variation having the greater versatility is the _____.

Standard Deviation
or Its Square, the Variance

130. The size of the range depends a good deal upon the size of the sample. There is more chance of simultaneously drawing a very high score and a very low score when the sample is larger. Consequently, the range generally increases with an increase in the size of the _____.

Sample

131. Because **all** the scores are used in computing the standard deviation, whereas only **two** scores (the **highest** and **lowest**) are used in computing the range, the standard deviation is much more stable than the range. The more stable measure of variability is the _____.

Standard Deviation

132. For example, a sample of 20 scores could be drawn at random from a population of 200 scores. The standard deviation and the range could then be calculated, and the 20 scores would be returned to the popula-

tion pile. If this process were repeated many times, the standard deviations would vary in size much _____ than would the range.

Less

133. If we are computing a standard deviation from the **entire population** of scores, we divide the SS by N before taking the square root. If the scores 1, 3, 4, 5, 7 have an SS of 20 and they are the entire population, we divide 20 by _____ and then take the square root. The result is _____.

5

2

134. The symbol for the population standard deviation is σ (a lower case Greek sigma). Sometimes, calculators label this σ_n or s_n. The formula can be written as

$$\sigma = \sqrt{\frac{SS}{N}} \, .$$

If $SS = 64$ and $N = 4$, $\sigma = $ _____.

$$\sigma = \sqrt{\frac{64}{4}} = \sqrt{16} = 4$$

135. Treat 0, 0, 4, 4 as a population and compute σ. _____

$$SS = 16 \qquad N = 4 \qquad \sigma = \sqrt{\frac{16}{4}} = 2$$

136. If the scores represent a sample and we are using that sample to **estimate** the population standard deviation, the denominator is $N - 1$ instead of N.

If the scores 0, 2, 2, 3, 8 represented results for five recovering cocaine-addicted subjects and we wanted to estimate the standard deviation for **all** such people, we would divide the SS by _____.

$$5 - 1 = 4$$

137. The symbol for an **estimate** of the population standard deviation based on a sample is s. Sometimes calculators label this σ_{n-1} or S_{n-1}.

$$s = \sqrt{\frac{SS}{N-1}}.$$

The scores 0, 2, 4, 4, 4, 4, 6, 6, 6 have an SS of 32 (recall Frames 104–107). Use the scores as a sample, and estimate the population standard deviation (compute s). _____

$$s = \sqrt{\frac{SS}{N-1}} = \sqrt{\frac{32}{8}} = 2$$

138. Treat the scores 1, 1, 5, 9, 9 as a sample. Compute SS and then s. _____ _____

$$SS = 64 \qquad s = 4$$

139. A measure of variability that is used more in advanced statistics is the variance. An **estimate** of the population variance is s^2. If $s = 3$, then an estimate of the population variance is $3^2 = 9$. For Frame 138, when s was 4, estimate the population variance. _____

$$s^2 = 4^2 = 16$$

140. An even more direct way of estimating the population variance from a sample is to divide the SS by $N-1$ and not take the square root in the first place.

$$\text{Estimate of variance} = s^2 = \frac{SS}{N-1}$$

For the scores 1, 3, 4, 5, 7 from Frame 112 where the SS was 20, compute s^2. _____

Estimated Variance = SS/N–1 = 20/4 = 5

Computer Quick Start

Computer entries in normal font
Output in bold normal font
Comments in bold italics font
For more help, see Appendix C

Data Description using MINITAB

Data File *demo.dat*	Program File *desc_mtb.pgm*	Program File Comments
0 1 6 0	READ 'demo.dat' C1-C4	*C1-C4 means*
2 1 4 0	NAME C1 'x' C2 'y' C3 'z' C4 'group'	*column 1 through*
2 2 3 1	DESC C1-C4	*column 4*
3 3 2 1		
8 7 0 1		

COMPUTER OUTPUT (IN PART) MTB > EXEC 'desc_mtb.pgm'
Executing from file: DESC_MTB.PGM
Entering data from file: DEMO.DAT
5 rows read.

	N	**MEAN**	**MEDIAN**	**TRMEAN**	**STDEV**	**SEMEAN**
X	**5**	**3.00**	**2.00**	**3.00**	**3.00**	**1.34**
Y	**5**	**2.80**	**2.00**	**2.80**	**2.49**	**1.11**
Z	**5**	**3.00**	**3.00**	**3.00**	**2.24**	**1.00**
GROUP	**5**	**0.600**	**1.000**	**0.600**	**0.548**	**0.245**

Comments:

*TRMEAN = TRimmed MEAN which means taking off the lowest and highest 5%,
(rounded to nearest integer) and taking the mean of the rest. STDEV = s. SEMEAN
= Standard Error of the MEAN (covered later).*

Data Description using SAS

Data File *demo.dat*	Program File *desc_sas.pgm*	Program File Comments
0 1 6 0	DATA;	*DATA; enables file handling*
2 1 4 0	INFILE 'demo.dat';	*too advanced for this book.*
2 2 3 1	INPUT x y z group;	*Enter the line as is.*
3 3 2 1	PROC UNIVARIATE;	*Enter ; at end of lines.*
8 7 0 1	RUN;	

COMPUTER OUTPUT (IN PART) SAS

Variable = X

Moments

N	5	Sum Wgts	5
Mean	3	Sum	15
Std Dev	3	Variance	9
Skewness	1.481481	Kurtosis	2.925926
USS	81	CSS	36
CV	100	Std Mean	1.341641
T:Mean = 0	2.236068	Pr> |T|	0.0890

Quantiles(Def = 5)

100% Max	8	99%	8
75% Q3	3	95%	8
50% Med	2	90%	8
25% Q1	2	10%	0
0% Min	0	5%	0
		1%	0

Range	8
Q3—-Q1	1
Mode	2

etc. for the rest of the variables

Comments:

USS = Uncorrected Sum of Squares (ΣX^2): CSS = Regular SS
Std Dev = s: CV = Coefficient of Variation = (s / mean) $\star$ 100
To be covered later are the Std Mean = Standard Error of the Mean
T:Mean=0
Pr> |T|
Percentiles (quantiles based on 100%)

Data Description using SPSS

Data File *demo.dat*	Program File *desc_sps.sps*	Program File Comments
0 1 6 0	DATA LIST	*DATA LIST starts the data*
2 1 4 0	File= demo.dat	*input. The FILE= line would*
2 2 3 1	FREE/ x y z group.	*often work with the file name*
3 3 2 1	DESC	*'demo.dat' but the path was*
8 7 0 1	VARS= ALL	*needed in my PC system.*
	/STATS= ALL.	*FREE/ causes the data to be*
		read in free form.
		Remember . at end of
		commands and leave a blank
		at beginning of all lines except
		for the first line of a command.

COMPUTER OUTPUT (IN PART) SPSS
Number of valid observations (listwise) =   5.00

Variable X

Mean	3.000	S.E. Mean	1.342
Std Dev	3.000	Variance	9.000
Kurtosis	2.926	S.E. Kurt	2.000
Skewness	1.481	S.E. Skew	.913
Range	8.000	Minimum	.000
Maximum	8.000	Sum	15.000

Valid observations -   5   Missing observations -   0

COMMENTS:
The Std Dev is s and the Variance is s^2.
S. E. Mean is the Standard Error of the Mean. It will be covered later. Kurtosis and Skewness are measures of the Kurtosis and Skewness covered much earlier. Their quantitative aspects and their Standard Errors are beyond this brief text.

OPEN BOOK QUIZ ON VARIABILITY
(Answer on page 184)

1. Compute *ss* for the distribution 2, 2, 6, 6. _____

2. Compute the s for the distribution 2, 2, 6, 6. _____

3. On the basis of Problem 2, and without doing any further calculations, what would be *s* for the distribution 3, 3, 7, 7? _____

4. Compute the range for the distribution 2, 2, 6, 6. _____

5. Which distribution below would have the larger *s*? _____

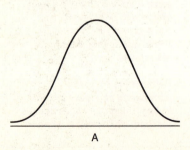

A   B

Inferential Statistical Methods

Probability

141. When faced with uncertainty such as tomorrow's weather, the outcome of a future spin of a roulette wheel, or the success of a shuttle mission, we use ideas of **probability.** The **probability** (or P) of an event is the proportion of time we think it might occur on the average, given what we know. If the probability of showers tomorrow is .60, for every 100 days when the winds, clouds, and so on appear to us as they appear today, we expect it to shower on about _____ of the following days.

---

60 (which is .60 * 100)

142. We will use probability ideas to answer two main types of questions. The first question is "What are the odds that some particular effect is simply due to chance?"

Example: We wonder whether drug X will increase long-term memory ability. We give a placebo to a control group and drug X to a test group. Suppose that the test group showed better long-term memory than the control group. The question now arises, "Could this much difference be due to chance, or is it more likely due to the effect of drug X?" We can get an answer to this by testing to see what the probability is that the difference could be **exactly** zero. This exact hypothesis is called the **null hypothesis.** "Null" means zero.

If this probability is very low, we are justified in rejecting the null hypothesis and accepting the alternate hypothesis that drug X probably makes a real difference. If we reject the null hypothesis, we have decided that the effect we witnessed (is, is not) due to chance. _____

Is Not

143. The second type of question is "What is the probable minimum value and maximum value in the population?"

Example: In the drug *X* example, instead of deciding merely whether the effect was probably due to chance or was due to drug *X,* we could make a statement such as "There is a 95 percent probability that the mean effect of drug *X* on long-term memory is between a lower boundary (LB) of an increase of two words to an upper boundary (UB) of eight words." In other words, we would be 95 percent sure that if the entire population from which we had sampled were to take drug *X,* their long-term memory superiority over a control group would probably be somewhere from two to eight words. This is called setting a **confidence interval.** In this example the 95 percent confidence interval of the mean extended from _____ to _____. We will discuss this later.

2   8

The Null Hypothesis

144. Consider a court of law. The jury is to approach a case with a predetermined hypothesis: that the guilt of the defendant is **exactly zero.** If nothing happens and no proof appears that the defendant is probably guilty, the jury simply retains this **hypotheses** or assumption of innocence. It is **NOT** necessary to prove that the defendant is innocent.

We'll use the symbol H_0 for this **null hypothesis** that the amount of guilt is **exactly zero.**

If we decide to reject the null hypothesis, we may then accept the **alternate hypothesis** that the amount of guilt is not zero.

	H_0 TRUE Person Is Innocent	H_0 FALSE Person Is Guilty
Reject H_0 (Find Defendant Guilty)	TYPE I ERROR (alpha error) (Innocent person convicted)	OK (power) 1 – beta (Guilty person convicted)
Retain H_0 (Find Defendant Not Guilty)	OK (Innocent person set free)	TYPE II ERROR (beta error) (Guilty person set free)

Human Decision

If the person is truly innocent, the H_0 is _______.

True

145. As in a court of law, in science the beginning hypothesis (called the **null hypothesis** and symbolized H_0) is: "The phenomenon or relationship does **not exist** (i.e. is exactly zero) in the population." Just as, in court, a prosecuting attorney could present evidence that would lead us to reject the assumption of innocence, so, in science, data can lead us to **reject the null hypothesis**. We then accept the **alternate hypothesis** that the phenomenon is present in the population.

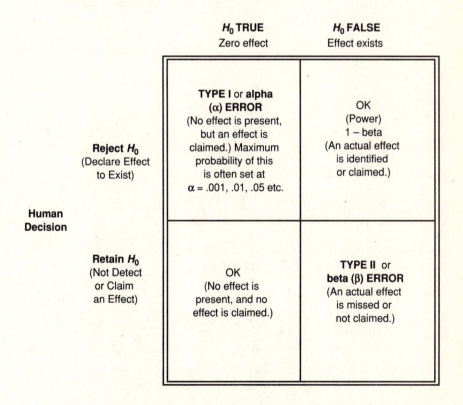

Human Decision	**H_0 TRUE** Zero effect	**H_0 FALSE** Effect exists
Reject H_0 (Declare Effect to Exist)	**TYPE I** or **alpha (α) ERROR** (No effect is present, but an effect is claimed.) Maximum probability of this is often set at α = .001, .01, .05 etc.	OK (Power) 1 – beta (An actual effect is identified or claimed.)
Retain H_0 (Not Detect or Claim an Effect)	OK (No effect is present, and no effect is claimed.)	**TYPE II** or **beta (β) ERROR** (An actual effect is missed or not claimed.)

Type I Error rate is often set at values like **.001, .01, .05** and is the maximum proportion of times H_0 is **rejected** out of all times when it is **true.** If there is no actual effect, the null hypothesis is _______.

True

146. When we reject H_0, the effect is said to be **significant.** This does **not** mean that it is important, but only that it probably is not due to chance. If we retain H_0, we are declaring the effect to be (significant, not significant). _____

Not Significant

147. When we use tables to determine the significance of some measure, such as a correlation coefficient, we choose some significance level, such as .05, and see whether the correlation that we have obtained can beat or at least match the tabled correlation. If it does, we declare our correlation to be significant at the .05 level. We are thus stating that the probability (P) that our correlation is due to chance is (less than or equal to, more than) .05. _____

Less Than or Equal to

Direct Probability

148. Two instances in which we get a probability (P) directly and do not need a table are:

1. Computer output where P is computed for us.
2. Some tests that actually generate a P.

The probability that the P refers to is for rejecting a null hypothesis when it is **true.** That type of error is called a Type _____ error.

I or Alpha

149. When P is low, it means that it is unlikely that an effect is due to chance alone. When chance becomes an unlikely explanation, it is reasonable to reject chance, and thus the null hypothesis, as the explanation of our results. Would we be most justified in rejecting the null hypothesis if P equaled .023 or .117? _____

.023

150. The probability of making a Type I error is also called **alpha** (α). When *P* is **below** some particular value (.05, .01, .001, etc.), the results are said to be **significant** at that level. If $P = .0276$, would the results be significant at the .05 level? _____ At the .01 level? _____

Yes   No

151. Person A says that she can control coin tosses with her mind and would like you to provide $1000.00 to stake her to a coin-tossing gambling game. If she makes money, she will give you half of whatever she makes. If she loses, you lose your $1000.00. She announces that, as proof of her ability, she will toss a coin three times and make it come up heads each time. She does so. The *P* of doing this by chance is one out of eight ($P = .5 \times .5 \times .5 = .125$, which is one out of eight).

Person B makes a similar offer, but as proof of her ability, she tosses a coin 20 times and it comes up heads each time. The *P* that this would happen by chance is one out of 1,048,576 ($P = 1/1,048,576 = .000000954$). Which person's result (A or B) is least likely to be by chance? _____ For which person would you be safest in rejecting the H_0? _____

If you were going to risk $1000.00 on anybody, on which person would you prefer to risk your money? _____

B, Because P Is So Small
B
B

152. The null hypothesis (H_0) is that a result is due to chance. It would be the best to retain the H_0 for person (A or B) _____ and reject it for person (A or B) _____.

A (More Likely Due to Chance)
B (*Less* Likely Due to Chance)

Laws of Probability

153. Two major concepts of probability are:

    1. The Additive law
    2. The Multiplicative law

    When the **additive** law is appropriate we **add** the probabilities. It applies when we say, "What is the probability of **EITHER** event A **OR** event B" when the events are **mutually exclusive.** A simple case: If P of a baby's being a male is .5 and P of the baby's being a female is .5, give P of being **EITHER** male **OR** female? _____

    $.5 + .5 = 1$

154. To get P for Event A **AND** Event B happening when they are **independent** of each other, use the **multiplicative** law. The figure below shows all possible rolls with two dice (each roll having a P of 1/36). Dice are different shades to tell them apart. Give P of the light die coming up 5 **AND** the darker die coming up 6. _____ Give P of the light die coming up 6 **AND** the darker die coming up 5. _____ If we can get an 11 by (light 6 **AND** dark 5) **OR** (light 5 **AND** dark 6), what is P of rolling 11 with two dice? _____

What is *P* of rolling 7? _____

$$1/6 * 1/6 = 1/36$$
$$1/6 * 1/6 = 1/36$$
$$1/36 + 1/36 = 2/36 \text{ (which reduces to 1/18)}$$
$$6/36 \text{ (which reduces to 1/6)}$$
since there are 6 ways to do it and we add them.

155. What is *P* of rolling 7 **OR** 11? _____

What is *P* of rolling 7 **AND THEN** 11? _____

$1/6 + 1/18 = 6/36 + 2/36 = 8/36 = 2/9$ **(Additive Law)**
$1/6 * 1/18 = 1/108$ **(Multiplicative Law)**

OPEN BOOK QUIZ ON PROBABILITY
(Answers on pages 184–185)

1. If an effect is significant at the .01 level, we have a 1 percent or lower chance of being wrong out of all cases in which _____.

2. If there is a .9 percent chance of making a correct decision about experiment A **and** the same chance for totally independent experiment B, what is the probability of being correct on both A and B?

3. In Problem 2, what is the probability of being correct about A and incorrect about B?

4. All things being equal, if alpha (probability of a Type I error) is lowered, what will happen to the probability of Type II errors?

5. If an experimenter is reluctant to make Type I errors, which alpha level should she use (.10, .05, .01, .001)?

Confidence Intervals

156. Up to this point, inferential methods have been used to:

1. Make point estimates of parameters (as means and standard deviations). **Remember, a parameter is the *population* value, while a statistic is a *sample* value.**
2. Make decisions about H_0.

The next example represents a class of inferential methods that yield upper and lower boundaries for intervals within which one can feel rather confident that a parameter lies.

If we wished to estimate the mean SAT score for a college and had only the resources to test a random sample of students, we might find that the best estimate was 525 (for example). We might additionally show that there was a 95 percent chance that the population mean was in the interval from 514 to 536 (for example). From earlier frames we know that this is called setting the _____ _____ of the mean.

Confidence Interval

157. To get some insight into this approach, consider the cases in the figure below as a population. Let us now take a random sample of four scores, compute their mean, and plot it on the *X* axis.

If the first sample of scores was 40, 50, 70, and 80, place an *X* where its mean would be on the line below:

	*	*		*	*	
20	30	40	50	60	70	80

				X		
20	30	40	50	60	70	80

158. In a similar manner, compute the mean and place an *X* on the line below for the means from each of these successive samples:

Sample Number	Hypothetical Values				Mean
1st	40	50	70	80	60
2nd	40	50	55	55	____
3rd	30	35	35	80	____
4th	45	45	50	60	____
5th	30	35	40	55	____

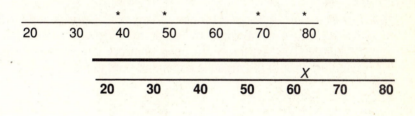

			X			
20	30	40	50	60	70	80

Since extreme values would tend to cancel out, the distribution of means should be (less, more) variable than the original distribution of single scores.

_____

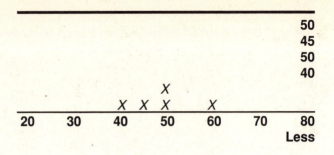

Standard Error of the Mean

159. The standard deviation of these means, called the **S**tandard **E**rror of the **MEAN,** is symbolized by $s_{\bar{x}}$ or by Std MEAN, S.E. MEAN, or SEMEAN. The last three are used primarily in computer output. The standard error of the mean is estimated from the formula

$$s_{\bar{x}} = \frac{s}{\sqrt{N}}$$

where s is the estimated standard deviation and N is the sample size. This relationship pops up in so many formulas and concepts that it may be to behavioral scientists what $e = mc^2$ is to physicists.
   In the present example, if $s = 10$ and $N = 4$,

$$s_{\bar{x}} = \frac{s}{\sqrt{N}} = \underline{\hspace{1cm}} / \underline{\hspace{1cm}} = \underline{\hspace{1cm}}$$

$$\frac{10}{\sqrt{4}} = 5$$

160. Compute the $s_{\bar{x}}$ for the visual perception scores given in Frame 103. They were 0, 2, 4, 4, 4, 4, 6, 6, 6. Recall that these nine scores had an s of 2 (Frame 137). _____

$$s_{\bar{x}} = 2/3 = .67$$

Distribution of Means

161. No matter what the shape of the original distribution is (skewed, bi-modal, rectangular, normal, etc.), a wondrous event occurs with the distribution of the means. As the size and number of samples increase, the distribution **approaches the normal distribution.** Since the mean of all the means would naturally approach the population mean, the theoretical distribution of means can be completely described.

With sample sizes equal to 4 and the population standard deviation equal to 10, the standard error of the means would equal _____, the mean of the means would equal _____, and the distribution would be close to _____.

5
50
Normal

162. Since the means approach being normally distributed, it follows that about 95 percent of the means would be within two standard errors of the population mean.

We do not have a large number of means. We have only our sample mean, and our need is not so much to know how sample means distribute, but how to use the values we have (MEAN, s, and N) to get an idea of how far away the population mean is likely to be from our particular sample _____.

Mean

The following medieval spy story may help:

Once upon a time there was a walled village named Gaussburg. Below is a map of the village and its 100 houses. In the center of the village was a famous mint. The large building marked M is the mint. Notice that about $2^1/2$ percent of the houses are more than 2 miles upstream from the mint and about $2^1/2$ percent are more than 2 miles downstream.

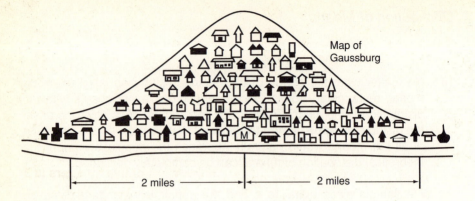

Map of Gaussburg

|←———— 2 miles ————→|←———— 2 miles ————→|

A roving band of numismatists from Würm wished to position a spy within 2 miles of the mint. Their problem was to determine how likely it was that the mint would be within 2 miles of any house chosen at random from the classified shouts of the town crier.

The map shows that 95 percent of the houses were within 2 miles of the mint. The entire band was puzzled about how to use this information until the very youngest numismatist piped up, "If 95 percent of the houses are within 2 miles of the mint, then won't the mint itself must be within 2 miles of 95 percent of the houses?"

Feeling 95 percent confident that the mint would be within 2 miles of any house they might randomly acquire, the numismatists finally had peace of mind. This period later came to be known as the "Peace of the Würm Mint Spy."

163. In other words, 95 percent of sample means (given that the sample size is moderately large) will fall within about two standard errors (2 $s_{\bar{x}}$) of the population mean, and you may thus feel 95 percent confident that, for any particular sample mean you might gather, the population mean is not more than about _____ standard errors away.

$$\overline{}$$
2

Degrees of Freedom

164. Let's take a timeout for an explanation of something called **degrees of freedom** (**df**). A story may help.

The poster reads, "Come one, come all. See Mental the Magnificent read minds." We sit in the darkened auditorium and ethereal music flows over the audience. Mental calls up a stranger and says, "Think of five numbers but don't tell them to me. What is their mean?" The stranger says "three." Mental touches the stranger's head with his hand and commands, "Now tell me only four of the numbers." The stranger says, "One, two, four, and five." Concentrating until beads of perspiration stand out on his head, Mental announces, "The fifth number you are thinking of is **three.**" The stranger gasps, "That's right!" and some of the audience break into applause. Strangely, however, some of the audience smile or laugh or even boo. What do they realize?

If the mean of five numbers is 3
then their total must be 15.
If four of the numbers are
1, 2, 4 and 5, which total up to 12,
then the last number is not free;
it must be 15 – 12 = 3.
Mental the Magnificent seems to be a fake.

165. If there are 9 numbers ($N = 9$) and we know their mean (or total), how many do we need to be told in order to know them all? This is the same as saying, "How many are free to be any number?" However many numbers are free is called the degrees of freedom (df).

---

df = 8 which is $N-1$ since the last number MUST be
the grand total minus the total of all the other numbers.
When only one variable is involved,
the degrees of freedom (df) is thus $N-1$.

Computing the Confidence Interval of the Mean

166. With small samples (below 20 or so) $s_{\bar{x}}$ and the sample means start to become erratic, so we have to cast the net somewhat farther than 2 $s_{\bar{x}}$ on each side of the sample mean to have some particular surety (such as 95 percent) of capturing the population mean. In this circumstance we compute $s_{\bar{x}}$ just as before, but instead of multiplying by 2, we multiply $s_{\bar{x}}$ by a special value (t) that depends on the sample size and the probability with which we want to be sure of catching the population mean. For example, if we wish to set boundaries that have a 95 percent chance of including the population mean, we could use the t table

(Table 2). We use the .05 table values because if we are allowing up to .05 or 5 percent error, we can be 95 percent sure that we are correct.

Table 2   .05 Values for the Distribution of t
(For more complete table, see Table D in Appendix A, page 165)

df (N − 1)	t
1	12.71
2	4.30
3	3.18
4	2.78
6	2.45
8	2.31
12	2.18
20	2.09
30	2.04
60	2.00
120	1.98
INFINITE	1.96

Let's return to the visual perception scores from before (0, 2, 4, 4, 4, 4, 6, 6, 6) which had an *N* of 9, an *SS* of 32, an *s* of 2, and a mean of 4.

Using Table 2, $df = N - 1 = 9 - 1 = 8$, and the *t* value for df = 8 is 2.31. Multiplying the $s_{\bar{x}}$ (.67) by *t* (2.31) from the table yields 1.55.

The mean of the population has a 95 percent probability of being within 1.55 of the sample mean. Since the sample mean is 4, the population mean has a 95 percent probability of being between 2.45 (4 − 1.55) and 5.55 (4 + 1.55). This interval from 2.45 to _____ is called the 95 percent **confidence interval** of the mean.

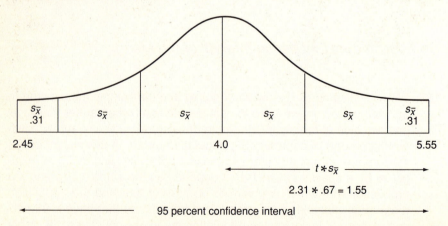

5.5

167. If for a sample of $N = 64$ the s is 16 and the mean is 10, an estimate of the standard error of the mean ($s_{\bar{x}}$) would be _____, and the nearest t for the 95 percent probability would be _____. Their product is _____. The confidence interval thus extends from _____ to _____.

$16/8 = 2$
2.0
4    $(10) - 4 = 6$
$(10) + 4 = 14$

168. Give the 95 percent confidence interval (CI) of the mean for the scores 0, 2, 2, 3, 8. These are the same scores that we used to learn how to compute the SS and later s. We can be 95 percent sure that the population mean lies between _____ and _____.

-0.73 6.73
Since the mean was 3, s was 3 and N was 5, then

$$s_{\bar{x}} = \frac{3}{\sqrt{5}} = 1.34.$$

t (from the .05 t table) for $N - 1$ or 4 degrees of freedom $= 2.78$.
The lower bound for the 95 percent CI of the mean was thus
$3 - (1.34 \times 2.78) = 3 - 3.73 = -0.73$.
The upper bound for the 95 percent confidence interval of the mean is $3 + (1.34 \times 2.78) = 3 + 3.73 = 6.73$.

Correlated t Test

169. Very little effort gives a useful extension. Suppose we are evaluating a technique for losing weight. The results for nine people are shown:

Before	After	Loss
130	130	0
132	130	2
128	124	4
115	111	4
140	136	4
130	126	4
130	124	6
136	130	6
160	154	6

Now ignore the Before and After scores, and look only at the Loss scores. They are **exactly** the same as the scores used earlier in setting confidence intervals. The only change is that now they represent weight loss scores.

Recall that we set a 95 percent CI of 2.45 to 5.55. We can thus be 95 percent sure that the true weight loss achieved by this method would be between _____ and _____ pounds

---

2.45   5.55

170. If we are 95 percent sure that the population (or true) weight loss is between 2.45 and 5.55 pounds, could we be at least 95 percent sure that we are correct if we reject the idea that this method produces no weight loss? _____

**Yes. If reality (the population value)
probably lies between 2.45 and 5.55,
then 0.0 is a rather remote possibility.
This way of using the standard error of the mean is
known as the correlated *t* test
or the dependent *t* test or the within subject *t* test.**

171. A company claims that it can tutor students who are going to take the verbal SAT and improve their scores. As proof, it offers data from a study in which it took carefully matched students and gave a randomly selected member of each matched pair the company's course. The results are:

Control Subject	Tutored Subject	Improvement
550	550	0
475	477	2
450	452	2
600	603	_____
500	508	_____

Give the 95 percent CI for improvement. _____ to _____.

3
8
−0.73 to 6.73

Mean gain was 3, $s_{\bar{x}} = 3/\sqrt{5} = 1.34$
t at the .05 level for 4 degrees of freedom = 2.78
Lower bound = 3 + (1.34 ∗ 2.78) = 3 − 3.73 = −0.73
Upper bound = 3 + (1.34 ∗ 2.78) = 3 + 3.73 = 6.73

172. If we can be sure only that the gain is between −0.73 (actually a loss) and 6.73, can we be sure that the true test gain is not zero?

_____

No. Zero is a very real possibility since there is a 95 percent chance that the population gain is between −0.73 and 6.73, an interval that includes zero.

OPEN BOOK QUIZ ON CONFIDENCE INTERVAL OF THE MEAN
(Answers on page 185)

1. Assume a sample of 64 scores with $\bar{X}$ of 90 and s of 4: Estimate the standard error of the mean.

2. What would be the appropriate value of t to use in setting up a 95 percent confidence interval for Problem 1? (*Hint:* If the df you need is not on the t table, use the next lowest df.)

3. For Problem 1, the upper and lower boundaries for the CI of the mean would lie _____ points from the mean.

4. Compute the lower and upper boundaries for the 95 percent confidence interval of the mean.
   Lower boundary (or limit) = _____
   Upper boundary = _____

5. What is the probability that the actual population mean lies outside the 95 percent confidence interval? _____

Correlation Coefficient: The Ups and Downs of Relationships

173. Many variables or events in nature are related to each other. As the sun rises, the day warms up; as children age, their thinking becomes more complex; and people who are bright in one area tend to be bright in others. Such relationships are called **correlations.** The relationship of one variable to another is known as a _____.

Correlation

174. If one variable tends to increase when the other increases, such as spending and wealth, the correlation is said to be positive. If one tends to increase when the other decreases, such as happiness and illness, they are said to be negatively correlated.

   If the river rises when it rains, the two events are said have a positive correlation. That is, when an increase in one variable coincides with an increase in another variable, the two variables have a _____ correlation.

Positive

175. Altitude and air pressure have a negative correlation. When an increase in one variable coincides with a decrease in another variable, the two variables have a negative correlation. With children, bedwetting and age usually have a _____ _____.

Negative Correlation

176. We can predict the occurrence of one event from another event, but we cannot say that one event **causes** the other event. There is a positive correlation between the number of drownings per day and the number of ice cream sales, but drownings do not cause the ice cream sales or vice versa. What third variable might cause these variables to be correlated? _____

Heat, Temperature

177. There must be a common link between the sets of variables being correlated. If two tests are to be correlated, the same person or people who take both tests must be matched on related variables. Could we correlate the performance of a fifth grade class on test A with the performance of an unmatched fifth grade class on test A? _____.

No

178. The most common numerical measure of correlation is called the **correlation coefficient,** symbolized by r. When we see r, it symbolizes the _____ _____.

Correlation Coefficient

179. The full name of the correlation coefficient about which we are learning here is the **Pearson product moment correlation coefficient.** However, over 90 percent of the time, you will use and hear simply **"the correlation"** or **"the correlation coefficient."** Just for practice, let's hear it all together this one time. The symbol r stands for the

_____ _____ _____ _____ _____.

Pearson Product Moment Correlation Coefficient

180. An r can range from +1.00 for a perfect positive linear (straight-line) relationship, through 0.00 for no linear relationship, to −1.00 for a perfect _____ linear relationship.

Negative

181. We have learned that when high values on one test tend to go with low values on another test, the tests are negatively correlated. The algebraic sign of minus (−) indicates a negative correlation or an inverse relationship. The algebraic sign of plus (+) indicates a positive correlation or a direct relationship. Which diagram illustrates inversely related variables having an $r = -1.00$? _____

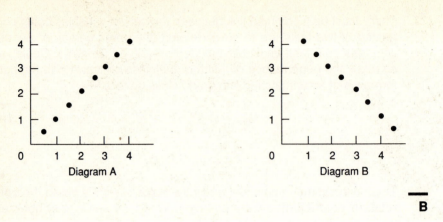

Diagram A   Diagram B

B

182. A correlation of −1.00 is just as strong a correlation as +1.00, and it is just as unlikely to occur by chance. The algebraic sign (+ or −) of *r* indicates the direction of the relationship (whether direct or inverse). It is the **absolute size of r** that indicates the strength or closeness of the relationship.

   Is an *r* of −0.80 stronger or weaker than an *r* of +0.60? _____

   Stronger
   |−0.80| > |+0.60| which is read "The absolute value of
   −0.80 is greater than the absolute value of +0.60"

183. The value *r* gives the degree to which the relationship between two variables can be represented by a **straight** line. Which of the variables in the diagrams below (*X, Y,* or *Z*) has the strongest *r* with the variable A? _____

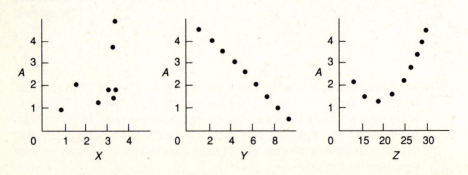

X   Y   Z

Y

184. In the real world it is common for the value of *r* to be less than −1.00 or +1.00. The more closely the dots approach a straight, thin line, the higher the *r*. Which of the variables (*X*, *Y*, or *Z*) has the highest *r* with the variable A? _____ Which has the lowest? _____

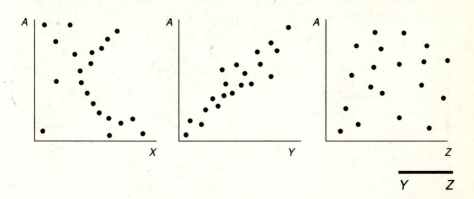

185. To get a feel for the closeness of relationship indicated by various sizes of *r* (all positive for easy comparison), compare the following graphs, and estimate the *r* of Graph E. _____

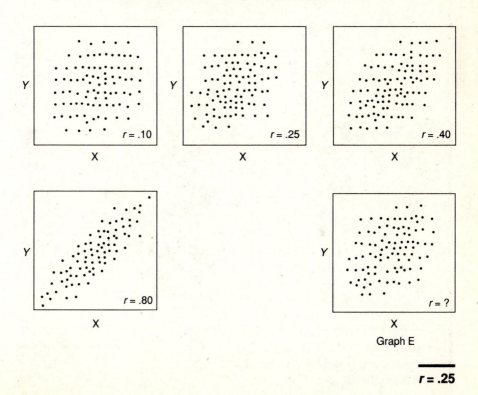

r = .25

Practical Computation

186. In computing the correlation coefficient, a value similar to the *SS* must be found; it is the sum of products (*SP*). The formula for the SP (to be explained below) is

$$SP = \Sigma XY - \frac{\Sigma X \Sigma Y}{N}$$

X represents the scores on the visual perception test. *Y* is the score on the reading test. Each *Y* score is multiplied by its corresponding *X* score. The products are then summed (ΣXY).

I Did This

X	Y		XY
0 * 2	=	0
2 * 3	=	6
4 * 2	=	8
4 * 4	=	16
4 * 7	=	28
4 * 8	=	32
6 * 4	=	24
6 * 7	=	42
6 * 8	=	48
ΣX	=	36
ΣY	=	45
ΣXY	=	204

You Try This

X	Y	XY
0	1	_____
2	1	_____
2	2	_____
3	3	_____
8	7	_____
$\Sigma X =$		_____
$\Sigma Y =$		_____
$\Sigma XY =$		_____

—
0
2
4
9
56
15
14
71

187. Note the similarity of the formula for the *SP* with that for the *SS*. With the *SS* it was the sum of all the *X* times *X* (i.e., itself) and then (ΣX) times (ΣX) in the CF. With the SP it is the sum of all the *X* times their respective *Y* and their ΣX) times (ΣX) in the CF.

I Did This

$$SP = \Sigma XY - (\Sigma X * \Sigma Y)/N$$

=204−(36*45)/9
=204−180
=24

You Try This

$$SP = \Sigma XY - (\Sigma X * \Sigma Y)/N$$

$SP =$ _____

= 71−(15 * 14)/5
= 29

188. The SS for Y (SS_y) will be needed and is computed in the same way as SS_x.

I Did This		You Try This	
Y	Y^2	Y	Y^2
2	4	1	_____
3	9	1	_____
2	4	2	_____
4	16	3	_____
7	49	7	_____
6	64		
4	16		
7	49		
_8_	_64_		
45	275		

$$SS_y = \Sigma Y^2 - (\Sigma Y)^2/N$$
$$= 275 - 45^2/9$$
$$= 50 \qquad SS_y = \text{_____}$$

1
1
4
9
_49_
$64 - 14^2/5 = 24.8$

189. A formula for r is:

$$r = \frac{SP}{\sqrt{SS_x\, SS_y}}$$

We collect the needed statistics from previous calculations.

I Did This	You Try This
$SP = 24$	$SP =$ _____
	(see Frame 181)
$SS_x = 32$	$SS_x =$ _____
	(see Frame 106)
$SS_y = 50$	$SS_y =$ _____
	(see Frame 182)

29.0
36.0
24.8

190

I Did This	You Try This
$r = \dfrac{SP}{\sqrt{SS_x\,SS_y}}$	
$r = \dfrac{24}{\sqrt{32 * 50}}$	
$= \dfrac{24}{\sqrt{1600}}$	
$= \dfrac{24}{40}$	
$= .600$	$r = \underline{\hspace{2cm}}$

$$= 29/29.880$$
$$= .971$$

191. A correlation coefficient is not a direct measure of the percentage of relationship between two variables. We cannot say that a correlation of +0.90 is three times as close a relationship as +0.30, but merely that it indicates a much higher degree of relationship. The correlation values or coefficients of correlation are not measurements on a scale of equal units. Are two tests having an r of +0.40 twice as related as two tests having an r of +0.20?

No

192. Whether a correlation is considered high or not depends on what we are correlating. Some predictions do not have to be very precise to be useful. As a result, even a small amount of correlation is noteworthy. Ignoring the **use** of a correlation, an overall rule of thumb for judging correlation size is to consider an r of 0.70 to 1.00 (either + or −) as a high correlation and an r of 0.20 to 0.40 as a relatively low correlation. Disregarding use, how would you describe a correlation of .35?

Low (or Relatively Low)

Interpretation of r^2

193. The square of r (r^2) has special importance. It is the proportion of the variance of one variable that can be predicted by the other.

     For example, if the r between the SAT verbal score and college grade point average (GPA) is .5, then $r^2 = $ _____. This means that .25 or 25 percent of the variability of scores on the GPA could be **predicted** by the qualities in the student measured by the SAT. The rest of the variability of score on the GPA remains unpredicted. That proportion is $1 - r^2$, which in this case is _____.

$.5^2 = .25$

$1 - r^2 = 1 - .25 = .75$ **or 75 percent**

194. This 75 percent could be due to such variables as acquiring or recovering from mono, breaking a leg, getting on or off some drug, getting in or out of financial difficulty, starting a constructive personal relationship or having a rocky time in a relationship, losing or acquiring purpose in life, and so on. For reasons given earlier, we have to be **very** cautious about confusing correlation and causation. That is why this text uses the term **predicted** instead of **explained** by. If r had been .6, the percent of GPA that could be **predicted** by the attributes measured by the SAT would be _____, and the percent *that could not be predicted* would be _____.

.36 or 36 percent

$1 - .36 = .64$ **or 64 percent**

195. Recall the degrees of freedom (df) discussion when we learned to set confidence intervals of the means (Mental the Magnificent). With one variable we used $N - 1$. With correlations, there are two variables, X and Y. If we know the means of X and Y and the r, only $N - 2$ pairs (where N is the total number of pairs), are free to vary. This is the df. What is the df for r between 20 pairs of scores? _____

---

df $= N - 2 = 20 - 2 = 18$

Significance of a Correlation Coefficient

196. You might want to know whether a correlation is large enough that you could feel fairly certain that the relationship was not just chance. That is, is the *r* of a sample large enough that it is very improbable (say, less than 5 percent) that the population *r* is 0.0? To put this another way, is the correlation significant at the .05 level? In Table 3 go down to the number of pairs minus 2 ($N - 2$). To reject the null hypothesis of no relationship in the population, the absolute value of your *r* **has to be as large as or larger than** the table or critical value. Using the following table, what is the critical *r* if df = 60? _____

Table 3   .05 Points for the Distribution of *r*
(For more complete table, see Table A in Appendix A)

$N - 2$ (Degrees of Freedom)	Critical *r*
1	.997
2	.950
3	.878
4	.811
6	.707
8	.632
12	.532
20	.423
30	.349
60	.250
120	.179

.250

197. In the earlier calculations of *r*, a sample of nine pairs of scores was found to have an *r* of .60. Would this indicate a probable non-zero correlation in the population? _____

No. With df = 9 − 2 = 7, the *r* needed would be somewhere between .632 and .707. With our computed *r* of only .60, we cannot reject luck as the explanation for the sample correlation.

198. Would an *r* of −.583 be significant at the .05 level if we had 22 subjects? _____

Yes.
−.583 beats the .423 needed at a df of 20 (from 22 − 2).

199. In the earlier practice problem that you did, *r* was .971 with five subjects. Is an *r* of .971 significant at the .05 level? _____

Yes.
.971 beats the critical value of .878 needed for significance when df = 5 − 2 = 3.

200. Compute *r* and test for significance. _____

X	Y
0	6
2	4
2	3
3	2
8	0

$r = -.9327$
Significant at the .05 level (beats .8783) but
not at the .01 level (fails to meet or beat .9587).
Notice that it was significant
even though it was negative.
It is the absolute value that counts.

Computer Quick Start

Computer entries in normal font
Output in bold normal font
Comments in bold italics font
For more help, see Appendix C

Correlation using MINITAB

Data File *demo.dat*	Program File *corr_mtb.pgm*	Program File Comments
0 1 6 0	READ 'demo.dat' C1-C4	
2 1 4 0	NAME C1 'x' C2 'y' C3 'z' C4 'group'	
2 2 3 1	CORR C1-C4	
3 3 2 1		
8 7 0 1		

COMPUTER OUTPUT
MTB > EXEC 'corr_mtb.pgm'
Executing from file: corr_mtb.pgm
Entering data from file: demo.dat
        5 rows read.

	X	Y	Z
Y	0.971		
Z	−0.932	−0.898	
GROUP	0.609	0.660	−0.816

Comments:

Intersections give the correlations. If we go down from x and across from y, we find 0.971, which is the correlation we got in Frame 184 with the same data.

Correlation using SAS

Data File *demo.dat*	Program File *corr_sas.pgm*	Program File Comments
0 1 6 0	DATA;	*DATA; enables advanced file*
2 1 4 0	INFILE 'demo.dat'	*handling beyond this book.*
2 2 3 1	INPUT x y z group;	*Remember ; at end of lines.*
3 3 2 1	PROC CORR;	
8 7 0 1	RUN;	

COMPUTER OUTPUT (IN PART)

Correlation Analysis
Pearson Correlation Coefficients / Prob > |R| under Ho: Rho =0 / N = 5

	X	Y	Z	GROUP
X	1.00000	0.97056	−0.93169	0.60858
	0.0	0.0060	0.0212	0.2761
Y	0.97056	1.00000	−0.89803	0.65991
	0.0060	0.0	0.0385	0.2255
Z	−0.93169	−0.89803	1.00000	−0.81650
	0.0212	0.0385	0.0	0.0917
GROUP	0.60858	0.65991	−0.81650	1.00000
	0.2761	0.2255	0.0917	0.0

Comments:

At the intersection of going across from one variable and down from the other is the correlation between the two variables. The intersection going across from Y and down from X gives 0.97056 as the r between the two. This corresponds to the r of 0.971 found in Frame 184. The 0.006 below the r is the probability that the absolute value of r (|R| above) would be greater than 0.97056 if the H_0 that the population correlation coefficient (called Rho) was 0.0 was true. This checks with our finding from the table that this probability was less than .01 (i.e., r was significant at the .01 level).

Correlation using SPSS

Data File *demo.dat*	Program File *corr_sps.sps*	Program File Comments
0 1 6 0	DATA LIST	*DATA LIST starts the data*
2 1 4 0	File= 'demo.dat'	*input. The FILE= line gives*
2 2 3 1	FREE/ x y z group.	*the file containing the data.*
3 3 2 1	CORR VARIABLES= ALL	*FREE/ causes data to be*
8 7 0 1	/STATS= ALL.	*read in free form.*
		Leave a blank at start of all
		lines but first of a
		command and notice . at end
		of command.

COMPUTER OUTPUT (IN PART)

- - Correlation Coefficients - -

	X	Y	Z	GROUP
X	1.0000	.9706	−.9317	.6086
	(5)	(5)	(5)	(5)
	P= .	P= .006	P= .021	P= .276
Y	.9706	1.0000	−.8980	.6599
	(5)	(5)	(5)	(5)
	P= .006	P= .	P= .038	P= .226
Z	−.9317	−.8980	1.0000	−.8165
	(5)	(5)	(5)	(5)
	P= .021	P= .038	P= .	P= .092
GROUP	.6086	.6599	−.8165	1.000
	(5)	(5)	(5)	(5)
	P= .276	P= .226	P= .092	P= .

(Coefficient / (Cases) / 2-tailed Significance)

Comments:

At the intersection of going across from one variable and down from the other is the correlation between the two variables. The intersection going across from Y and down from X gives 0.9706 as the r between the two. This corresponds to the r of 0.971 found in Frame 184. The 0.006 below the r is the P that the absolute value of r would be greater than 0.9706 if the H₀ that the population correlation coefficient was 0.0 were true. This checks with our finding from the table (when we were back in the text) that this P was less than .01 (i.e., r was significant at the .01 level).

OPEN BOOK QUIZ ON CORRELATION COEFFICIENT
(Answers on pages 184–185)

1. If grades tend to rise as class attendance increases, one could say that grades and attendance are _____ _____.

2. Which of the following represents the greatest *r*?

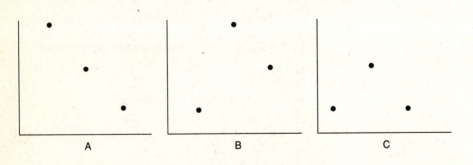

A   B   C

3. Comment on the assertion that a rise in relationship as *r* increases from .5 to .6 is equal to that when *r* increases from .7 to .8. _____

_____

4. Compute *r* for the following pairs of scores. _____

	X	Y
Ima	1	1
Lil	2	3
Dot	3	2

5. Compute *r* for the following pairs of scores. _____

	X	Y
Don	1	2
Ray	2	3
Joy	3	1

Regression

Consider a common need in our society: prediction. Companies want to predict which applicants will become good sales managers. Colleges and universities want to select the applicants who will profit most from studying at their institutions. People want to know tomorrow's weather today. Investors want to know what the stock market will be doing in the future. Prediction is a vital part of modern life.

Linear Equation

201. Before plunging into the ideas of prediction using regression analysis, we should, just to play it safe, review the simple linear equation.

Suppose that Pam has already driven 240 miles. If she drives two more hours at 60 miles per hour, how many total miles will she have driven?

_____

240 + (60 ∗ 2) = 240 + 120 = 360 miles

202. We can graph this, putting hours on the *X* axis and total mileage for Pam on the *Y* axis:

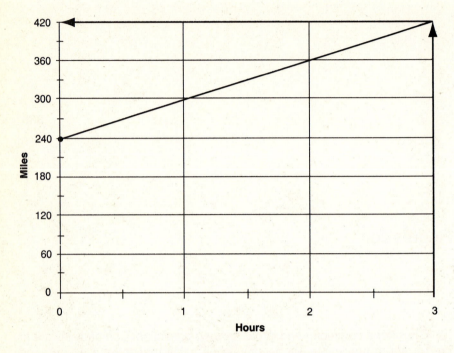

What will be the total mileage if Pam drives three more hours?

_____

_____

240 + (60 ∗ 3) = 240 + 180 = 420 miles

203. The number of units of change in *Y* divided by the number of units of change in *X* is called the **slope.** When someone says: "That car must have been going 85 miles per hour!" he or she is using a slope. For Pam the slope was _____.

60

Symbols

204. And now some symbols to go with the ideas:

Statisticians use different symbols than mathematicians. Don't worry if the symbols are not consistent with those used in any math you have taken.

For the predicted Y we use Y_{pred}, also commonly written as $\hat{Y}$, which is called "Y hat."

For the starting point of Y where X = 0, we use a. Thus a for Pam was _____. For the slope we use b, so b for Pam was _____.

X is the number of units of the predictor variable. In the first question about Pam, X = _____ and Y_{pred} is the predicted value for Y. In the first example when Pam drove two more hours, Y was _____ miles.

---

240   60
                  2
               360

205. Putting this all together, since we used predicted total miles $[Y_{pred}]$ = How far Pam had driven when we started counting [a] + (miles per hour [b] * hours driven [X]), we can use the symbols $Y_{pred} = a + bX$.

Just for practice, if you started out with $20.00 and worked 3 hours at $10.00 per hour, fill in the blanks to predict your wealth after the 3 hours.

Y_{pred} = a   + b   * X

_____ = _____ + _____ * _____

---

50 = 20 + 10 * 3

206. Remember that Y_{pred} represents the **predicted** Y. In the Pam example, that would be the number of miles from the station after X hours. a represents the value of Y at the point where X (hours) = 0. In this example a, called the Y intercept, was 240. b represents the slope, the rise in Y for each increase of one unit in X (60 miles for each hour driven in this problem). Compute Y_{pred} if X = 2: _____. Compute Y_{pred} if X = 3: _____.

---

240 + (60 * 2) = 360
240 + (60 * 3) = 420

207. In day-to-day practice, regression values are usually expressed in the most available units. Assume a freshman mean grade of 80 for all stu-

dents with a σ of 6, and assume that the mean SAT Verbal score in this school was 500 with a σ of 100 and a slope of .03. The figure might look as shown here. What would be the best grade estimate for an applicant with an SAT Verbal score of 700? _____.

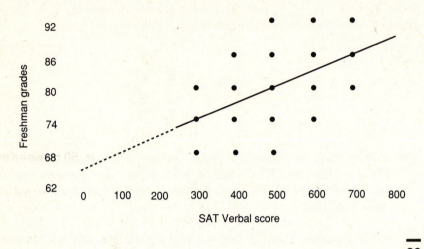

SAT Verbal score

—
86

208. Since predicted grades start at 65 and climb 3 grade points for every 100 SAT points (i.e., .03 grade points for every SAT point), the best estimate for freshman grades in this particular example may be obtained by

$$65 + .03 \times \text{SAT Verbal}$$

   If a student's SAT Verbal score is 200, what specific numbers would go with each symbol?

   $X =$ _____ $a =$ _____ $b =$ _____ $Y_{pred} =$ _____

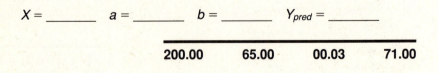

| 200.00 | 65.00 | 00.03 | 71.00 |

209. Note that a, the value on the Y axis, is 65 when it crosses above the point where $X = 0$. From that point, grades soar 3 points for each rise

of 100 SAT points (that is, .03 to 1). The predicted grade for an applicant with an SAT Verbal score of 600 is

$$65 + .03\,(600) = 65 + 18 = 83.$$

What is it for an SAT Verbal score of 500? _____?

80

210. Suppose that we are trying to predict college freshman GPAs from the SAT Verbal taken during the senior year of high school. For our purposes, assume that the *r* (the correlation coefficient) is .50 between the SAT Verbal score and freshman grades. Thus, on the average, a person with a relatively high SAT Verbal score would tend to earn relatively (high or low) freshman GPAs if he went to college with the same group to which he was compared when his relative standing on the SAT Verbal score was determined. _____

High

211. There is an interesting, curious, and fundamental relationship between predictor values and the actions one tries to predict. The predicted actions regress toward more **typical** (on the average) than the actions used as predictors. Those who have very low values on the predictor will regress toward the mean future performance and thus improve. Those who do unusually well on the predictor also regress toward the mean future performance and thus average (better or worse) in the future performance than on the predictor. _____

Worse

212. The principle is general. A group of men who are selected because they are very tall would tend to have sons who, when mature, would be closer to the mean of the general population and thus be shorter than the selected group. Men selected for shortness would tend to have sons who were (shorter or taller) than themselves. _____

Taller

213. In the following figure, SAT Verbal scores and grades have been converted to z scores. The mean freshman grade of all those having an SAT Verbal z score of +2 is _____.

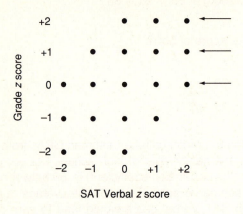

SAT Verbal z score

___
+1

214. Because the figure is symmetrical, one might have supposed that the best match for a +2 on the SAT Verbal score would be a +2 on freshman GPAs. Instead, the **best** estimate regressed closer to the mean. Fill in the missing values in the table below.

SAT Verbal z Score	Average z Score for Freshman with that SAT
+2	1.0
+1	_____
0	_____
−1	_____
−2	_____

___
+0.5
0.0
−.5
−1.0

215. Connecting these points yields the figure shown here. Notice that the line ascends .5 unit for every unit it moves to the right. This is called a .5 slope. The line is called a **regression line,** and its **slope** is called a

regression coefficient. The accompanying figure demonstrates a regression coefficient of _____.

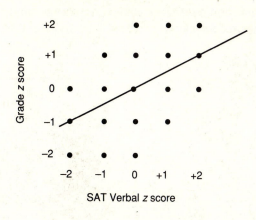

_____
.5

---

216. This example was arranged to teach some particular points about **regression.** In actual practice, the points would not be so **symmetrical,** and we probably could not figure out the *best* line for prediction by such easy inspection. There are, however, convenient formulas that let us decide on the very *best* line for predicting. We need to know how many units *Y* changes for each unit of change in *X*. This is called

_____.

_____
Slope

---

217. If we know nothing about a student, the best estimate of his or her freshman GPA *z* score is zero (the mean for all freshmen). Each s of the SAT Verbal score allows us to venture another .5s away from a grade estimate of zero. What would be the best estimate of the freshman grade *z* score for an applicant with an SAT Verbal *z* score of +3?

_____

_____
1.5

218. The general regression formula, when z scores are used, is $Z_{pred} = \beta * Z_x$, where Z_{pred} is the best estimate for the z score variable being predicted.

   β (read "beta") is the regression coefficient based on z scores (and thus called the normalized regression coefficient), and z_x is the z score of the predictor variable.
   In the preceding frame, $Z_{pred} =$ _____, $\beta =$ _____, and $Z_x =$ _____.

1.5   .5   3

Relationship to r

219. When there is just one X and one Y, the **normalized regression coefficient (β) and r are identical.** Thus, if two tests had an r of .8, for each standard deviation that an individual departed from the mean on one test, we would predict that he or she would move _____ standard deviations away from the mean on the other test.

.8

220. If the r between SAT Verbal scores and freshman GPAs were .4, we could best predict that an applicant having an SAT Verbal z score of -2 would have a freshman GPA z score of _____.

−.8

221. Which of the following scatter plots reflects the highest normalized regression coefficient? _____ Which represents the highest r?

_____

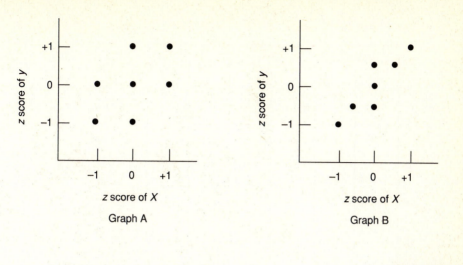

Graph A

Graph B

B   B

Least Squares Criterion

222. You might well wonder: "What is BEST about the line of **best fit?**" The criterion of **best** that is most commonly used in statistics is that we **choose a line to minimize the squares of the vertical deviations of the actual data from the prediction line.**

Well, there's a mouthful! The idea is important; let's break it down. Consider three subjects with the following scores:

	X	Y
Ann	0	0
Bob	2	4
Clo	4	2

Fill in the dots for a scatter plot.

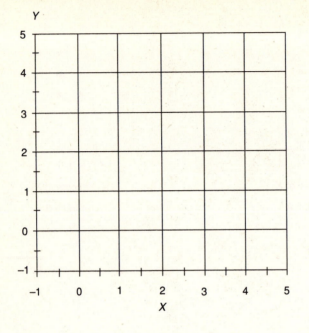

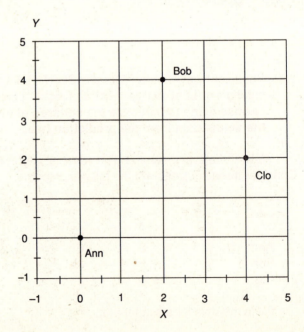

223. Consider two lines as candidates for **best predictors.**

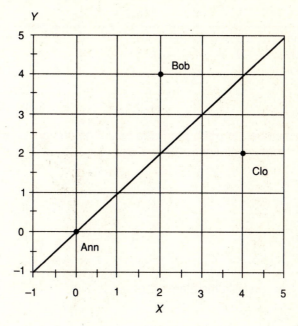

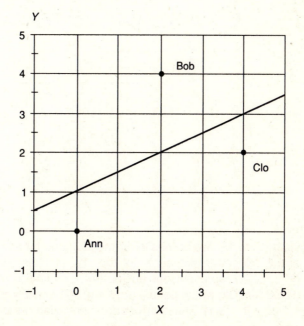

Using Line K:

	X	Y	Y_{pred}	$Y - Y_{pred} =$ residual	
Ann	0	0	0	$0 - 0 =$	0
Bob	2	4	2	$4 - 2 =$	2
Clo	4	2	_____	$2 - 4 =$	_____

Remember, to get a predicted value, go straight *up* from X until you hit the line; then go straight *over* to Y axis.

$$\overline{}$$

4   −2

224. Now you fill in the blanks for Line L:

	X	Y	Y_{pred}	$Y - Y_{pred} =$ residual
Ann	0	0	_____	_____
Bob	2	4	_____	_____
Clo	4	2	_____	_____

1   1
2   2
3   1

225. Go back to the two graphs in Frame 223, and for each subject, draw an arrow from the actual Y to the Y_{pred}. These vertical distances, $(Y - Y_{pred})$, represent our errors. For example, using line L, we predicted that Clo would get a 3 on Y, but she actually got a 2. Our error is -1 $(2 - 3 = -1)$. These errors are also called **residuals.**

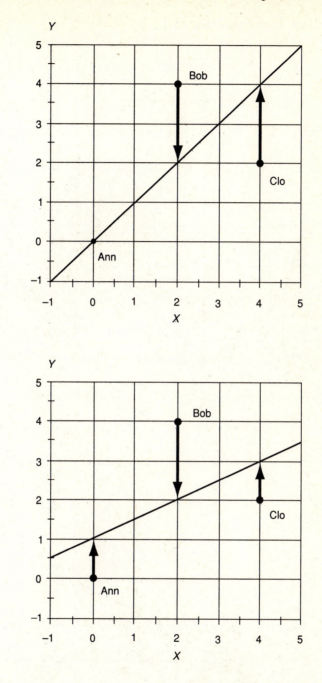

226. Our errors, the vertical deviations ($Y - Y_{pred}$) or residuals are like the residue that is left at the bottom of a cup of coffee. They are what's left

after we take our best shot at predicting Y using a straight line. Square
the residuals (errors) and fill in the blanks below.

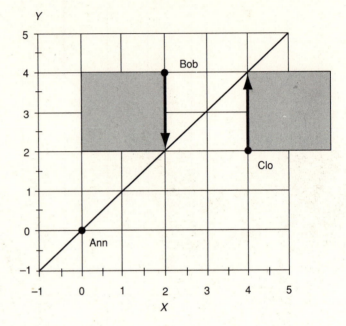

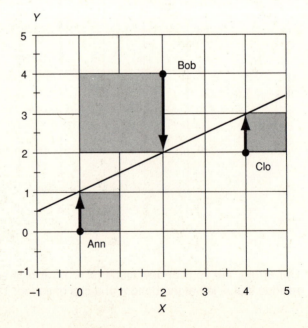

	Line K			Line L	
	$Y - Y_{pred}$	$(Y - Y_{pred})^2$		$Y - Y_{pred}$	$(Y - Y_{pred})^2$
Ann	0	0	Ann	−1	_____
Bob	2	4	Bob	2	_____
Clo	−2	4	Clo	−1	_____

1
4
1

227. After squaring these vertical deviations, we can sum the squares. For Line K this is 0 + 4 + _____ = _____.

4   8

228. What is the sum of the squared residuals for Line L? _____

1 + 4 + 1 = 6

229. Which of the prediction lines is the better of the two by the **least squares criterion?** _____

The last few frames were to show the idea of the least squares criterion. Proposing lines and comparing them is NOT how we actually get the best line out of all possible lines. A few simple formulas, which you will soon learn, let us define the best line. Recall that to define a line we need only compute the Y intercept (symbol is _____) and the slope (symbol is _____).

L, because 6 is less than 8
a
b

230. Just as r was called **linear** because a straight line was involved, the regression discussed in this program is called **linear regression.**

Prediction is usually improved by simultaneously using several, or multiple, variables to predict one variable. The technique is called multiple _____ regression.

Linear

231. The regression line has a formula that, if known and applied, can be used with varying success to predict anything, once a predictor's relationship to the predicted is known. Recall that if we had some values called a and b, we could take any particular X and predict Y (compute Y_{pred}) by the formula $Y_{pred} = a + bX$. The equation of the line using raw data involves a constant (a) plus a _____ coefficient (b) for the predictor variable times an individual score (X).

Regression

232. As an example of how a regression analysis might be used to predict behavior, suppose that an admissions director for a college wanted to predict the performance of students in their freshman year. She would first get, for example, the SAT scores of a group of students (the X scores) and follow up by getting the grade point averages for that same group (the Y scores). From these pairs of X and Y scores she could compute values for a and b. Now let us suppose that a student applies for admission. If the director had that student's SAT score (X), she could get a prediction of that student's grade point average (Y_{pred}) by the formula _____.

$Y_{pred} = a + bX$

233. Here are the original data from frames 180 to 184. Compute SP, SS_x, SS_y, and the means for X and Y just as before, but now it should take much less time.

I Did This		You Try This	
X	Y	X	Y
0	2	0	1
2	3	2	1
4	2	2	2
4	4	3	3
4	7	8	7
4	8	SP	= ____
6	4	SS_x	= ____
6	7	Mean of $X =$ ____
6	8	Mean of $Y =$ ____
SP	$=24$		
SS_x	$=32$		
Mean of $X = 5$			

29
36
3
2.8

Predicting Behavior: Practical Computations

234. With the *SP*, the SS_x (we don't need SS_y here) and the means for *X* and *Y* in hand, calculating *a* and *b* is easy.

$$b = SP/SS_x$$

I Did This	You Try This
$b = 24/32$ $= .75$	$b = \underline{\hspace{2em}}/\underline{\hspace{2em}}$ $= \underline{\hspace{2em}}$

$29/36 = .8056$

235

$$a = \overline{Y} - (b * \overline{x})$$

I Did This	You Try This
$a=5-(.75*4)$ $= 2$	$a=$ $\underline{\hspace{2em}} - (\underline{\hspace{2em}} * \underline{\hspace{2em}})$ $= \underline{\hspace{2em}}$

$.3833 + (.8056 * 4)$
$= .3833 + 3.2224$
$= 1.235$

236. Let us assume a predictor (*X*) score of 4 for the individuals whose *Y* scores are being predicted in both the example and the practice problem.

To predict *Y*, use $Y_{pred} = a + bX$. For a particular individual, add *b* times that subject's *X* score to *a*.

I Did This	You Try This
$Y_{pred}=a+bX$ $=2+(.75*4)$ $=2+3$ $=5$	$Y_{pred}=$ $\underline{\hspace{2em}}+(\underline{\hspace{2em}} * \underline{\hspace{2em}})$ $= \underline{\hspace{2em}} + \underline{\hspace{2em}}$ $= \underline{\hspace{2em}}$

$.3833 + (.8056 * 4)$
$= .3833 + 3.2224$
$= 3.606$

237. In summary, consider what we have just done in the example problem. Having gathered data from a sample of 5 subjects, we derived a regression equation. It was $Y_{pred} = .3833 + .8056 * X$. Along comes a subject with an X score of 4. We were able to use the prediction equation and predict that her Y score would be _____. Give Y_{pred} if her X score had been zero. _____ The MEAN of X was 3 and the MEAN of Y was 2.8. Predict Y if X = 3. _____

3.606
.3833
2.8

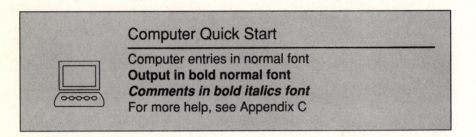

Computer Quick Start

Computer entries in normal font
Output in bold normal font
Comments in bold italics font
For more help, see Appendix C

Regression using MINITAB

Data File *demo.dat*	Program File *regr_mtb.pgm*	Program File Comments
0 1 6 0	NOBRIEF	***NOBRIEF causes maximum***
2 1 4 0	READ 'demo.dat' C1 C2	***output. The 1 in the line***
2 2 3 1	NAME C1 'x' C2 'y'	***Regress C2 on 1 C1 is the***
3 3 2 1	REGRESS C2 ON 1 C1;	***number of predicators. It is***
8 7 0 1	PREDICT 4.	***necessary. The semicolon at***
		the end of the REGRESS LINE
		indicates that a subcommand
		follows. The subcommand,
		PREDICT 4. is optional. In the
		text, the same data were used
		and the task was to predict Y if
		X = 4. The subcommand must
		end with a dot (.).

COMPUTER OUTPUT (IN PART) USING MINITAB
MTB > exec 'regr_mtb.pgm
Executing from file: regr_mtb.pgm
Entering data from file: demo.dat
5 rows read.

The regression equation is
y = 0.383 + 0.806 x

Predictor	Coef	Stdev	t-ratio	p
Constant	0.3833	0.4646	0.83	0.470
x	0.8056	0.1154	6.98	0.006

s = 0.6926   R-sq = 94.2%   R-sq(adj) = 92.3%

Analysis of Variance

SOURCE	DF	SS	MS	F	p
Regression	1	23.361	23.361	48.71	0.006
Error	3	1.439	0.480		
Total	4	24.800			

Obs.	x	y	Fit	Stdev.Fit	Residual	St.Resid
1	0.00	1.000	0.383	0.465	0.617	1.20
2	2.00	1.000	1.994	0.331	−0.994	−1.63
3	2.00	2.000	1.994	0.331	0.006	0.01
4	3.00	3.000	2.800	0.310	0.200	0.32
5	8.00	7.000	6.828	0.655	0.172	0.77

Fit	Stdev.Fit	95% C.I.	95% P.I.
3.606	0.331	(2.554, 4.657)	(1.163, 6.048)

Comments:

The Constant referred to above (.3833) is the Y intercept (a). The .8056 after x is the slope (b). The s is the same as the Root MSE (the square root of the MS for Error. The p of .006 says that there are just six chances in a thousand of predicting this well if only chance was involved.

R-sq(adj) is a more conservative estimate of the proportion of the variability of Y we can predict from X. The simple r^2 is an overstatement since the scores used to test the equation were the same scores used to derive the equation. The Fit column is y_{pred}. Stdev.Fit is the s of the Fit scores for a particular x. Residual = y − y_{pred} and is thus the amount and direction by which reality (y) differed from our prediction (y_{pred}). St.Resid = Residual scores converted to z scores. It stands for Standardized Residuals. The last line discusses y_{pred} if x = 4 since that was the x used in the text. The 95% C.I. is the Confidence Interval for the mean of all y scores where x = 4. The 95% P.I. is the Prediction Interval for all individuals who have x = 4. If Fran got a 4 on the predictor, we can be 95% sure ahead of time that her y score will be between 1.163 and 6.048.

Regression using SAS

Data File	Program File	Program File Comments
demo.dat	*regr_sas.pgm*	

0 1 6 0	DATA;	*DATA; enables file handling*
2 1 4 0	INFILE 'demo.dat';	*beyond this book. Just enter*
2 2 3 1	INPUT x y;	*the line as is. Remember ; at*
3 3 2 1	PROC reg;	*end of lines.*
8 7 0 1	MODEL y = x;	
	RUN;	

COMPUTER OUTPUT (IN PART) USING SAS

The SAS System

Dependent Variable: Y

Analysis of Variance

Source	DF	Sum of Squares	Mean Square	F Value	Prob > F
Model	1	23.36111	23.36111	48.707	0.0060
Error	3	1.43889	0.47963		
C Total	4	24.80000			

Root MSE	0.69255	R-square	0.9420
Dep Mean	2.80000	Adj R-sq	0.9226
C.V.	24.73403		

Parameter Estimates

Variable	DF	Parameter Estimate	Standard Error	T for H0: Parameter = 0	Prob > |T|
INTERCEP	1	0.383333	0.46457866	0.825	0.4698
X	1	0.805556	0.11542550	6.979	0.0060

Comments:

Generally the same as for MINITAB. SAS can give Residual information, but that was cut to save space.
The Y intercept is here labeled INTERCEP.
C.V. (Coefficient of Variation) is 100 times Root MSE divided by the mean.
$(100 \times (.69255/2.8000)) = 24.73403$.
This gives a measure of variability free of arbitrary units.

Regression using SPSS

Data File demo.dat	Program File regr_sps.sps	Program File Comments
0 1 6 0	DATA LIST	*DATA LIST starts the data*
2 1 4 0	File= 'demo.dat'	*input. The FILE= line gives*
2 2 3 1	FREE/ x y z group.	*the file containing the data.*
3 3 2 1	REGR VARIABLES= x y	*FREE/ causes data to be*
8 7 0 1	/DEPENDENT= y	*read in free form.*
	/METHOD= ENTER.	
		Leave a blank at start of all
		lines except first of a
		command and notice . at end
		of command.

COMPUTER OUTPUT (IN PART) SPSS

* * * * M U L T I P L E   R E G R E S S I O N * * * *

Multiple R	.97056		
R Square	.94198	R Square Change	.94198
Adjusted R Square	.92264	F Change	48.70656

Analysis of Variance

	DF	Sum of Squares	Mean Square
Regression	1	23.36111	23.36111
Residual	3	1.43889	.47963
F = 48.70656	Signif F =	.0060	

Variables in the Equation

Variable	B	SE B	95% Confdnce	Intrvl B	Beta
X	.805556	.115425	.438225	1.172886	.970557
(Constant)	.383333	.464579	-1.095142	1.861808	

Comments:

Generally same as for MINITAB. The B for X is our b. The (Constant) is our a. The Beta is the normalized regression coefficient that was noted as being the same as r when there is only one X and one Y.

Since Beta = .970557, that must be the value of r and you may note that this is equivalent to the r of .9706 between x and y that we saw in the Quick Start section on correlation.

The use of the SE B and 95% Confdnce Intrvl B are beyond this book but have to do with setting a confidence interval within which we can feel 95% confident that the population a and b lie.

Note that the significance level of our ability to predict y from x (P or Signif F = .0060) is exactly the same as the P for the r noted in the Quick Start section on correlation. It is equivalent to ask how well we can predict y from x (or x from y) and how sure we are that x and y have a population r that is not zero.

References to Multiple Regression and Multiple R are beyond this book but have to do with the idea that we can try to predict Y by several predictors used simultaneously. We could, for instance, try to predict College GPA by SAT scores and High School GPA. The single best predictor would enter the equation first and the second best next. The change references above have to do with how useful adding each new variable is. With only one variable, the change is simply comparing our predictor (x) with no predictor.

OPEN BOOK QUIZ ON REGRESSION
(Answers on page 186)

1. If the correlation between two variables was .6, a rise of 2 *z* score points in the *X* variable would cause one to predict a rise in the Y variable of _____ *z* score points.

2. Consider the following set of scores:

X	Y
0	0
2	4
4	2

Calculate b. _____

3. Calculate a. _____

4. Predict Y (i.e., compute Y_{pred}) if X = 4. _____

5. For which of the following scatter diagrams would a regression analysis (as we have studied it) be most appropriate? _____

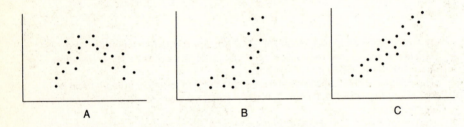

A   B   C

Analysis of Variance (ANOVA)

238. It is common to test to see whether the separate means of **several** groups differ significantly from each other. The technique for making this determination is called **analysis of variance** (abbreviated **ANOVA**). **Variance** is the square of the standard deviation. The variance of a population having a standard deviation of 3 is _____.

—
9

239. A typical ANOVA problem might involve randomly sampling subjects from a population of hyperactive boys. We will refer to these boys as the **subjects,** or Ss. We randomly divide the subjects into two groups. The second group is given the drug **Ritalin** every day for a month. The first group is given a **placebo** (a pill that looks like Ritalin but has no active ingredients). A psychiatrist who does not know which subjects got which pill evaluates the hyperactivity of the subjects at the end of the month with the following results:

Placebo	Ritalin
8	0
7	2
5	2
4	4

What is the mean for the placebo group? _____
For the Ritalin group? _____
What is the sum of squares (SS) for all eight subjects? _____

6
2
50

240. The SS of 50 represents the **total** variability of all the subjects. Assuming that Ritalin has **no** effect, the SS could be used to make inferences about the variability of the original population, but that is not what we are up to here.

   Using ingenious techniques to be learned later, we can, assuming that the null hypotheses is true, estimate the variability for the population by using the variability **within** the groups and also by using the variability **between** the groups. Total variability is thus broken down to variability between and variability _____.

Within

241. While the measure of variability at this stage is the SS, dividing a sum of squares by its degrees of freedom (df) gives an estimate of variance. Recall that on the way to getting s, an estimate of the standard deviation, we divided the SS by $N - 1$, the df, giving the variance estimate, s^2, and then got s by taking the _____ _____.

Square Root

242. Just how to get the proper df's will be covered shortly. In each case, SS/df equals an estimate of the _____.

Variance

243. If the null hypothesis is true (i.e., the effect of Ritalin is exactly zero), we would expect the estimates of the population variance based on both the **between group** variability and the **within group** variability to be (about equal, quite different) _____.

About Equal

Symbols

244. Remember that we could compute the population standard deviation by

$$\sigma = \sqrt{\frac{SS}{N}}\ .$$

Squaring this gives the population variance:

$$\sigma^2 = \frac{SS}{N}\ .$$

We are taking the **sum of squares** and dividing it by the **number** of squares that we summed. What do we call the sum of some values divided by the N of those values? _____

The Mean

245. Thus another way of looking at the variance is to call it the **mean square** (**MS**). An estimate of the variance based on the variability between groups can thus be labeled the **MS between groups** or MS_{bg}. How could you label the MS within groups? _____

MS Within Groups or MS_{wg}

246. There is the $MS_{between\ groups}$, or MS_{bg}, and the $MS_{within\ groups}$, or MS_{wg}. As was mentioned above, if the H_0 is true, we expect the MS_{bg} to be equal to the MS_{wg}. When we expect two values to be equal, we would expect one of them divided by the other, on the average, to equal

_____.

1.0

247. The ratio of the MS_{bg} divided by the MS_{wg} is given a special name, the **observed F,** or simply F. When H_0 is true, we expect F to be _____.

1.0

248. Even when H_0 is true, sampling variability would cause the Fs to vary from 1. If it were too much more than 1.0, we might begin to suspect that there was more to the MS_{bg} than just random sampling variability. There might be variability between groups due to the effect of Ritalin. If there were a Ritalin effect, the H_0 would be (true, false). _____

False

249. When H_0 is true, the MS_{bg} and MS_{wg} both reflect random sampling variability. If H_0 is false, MS_{wg} still reflects only random sampling variability but the MS_{bg} reflects random sampling **plus** a Ritalin effect.

We would now, with H_0 false, expect the MS_{bg} to be (larger, the same, smaller) than the MS_{wg}. _____

Larger, (random + Ritalin) for the MS_{bg} as compared with just random for the MS_{wg}.

250. If there is a true Ritalin effect then we would expect F to be (less than 1, 1, greater than 1). _____

Greater Than 1

251. One problem now would be: How big does F have to get before we become convinced that there is more to the MS_{bg} than just the random sampling effect? Tables exist to tell us. For example, using methods that we'll soon learn, for the Ritalin experiment the $MS_{bg} = 32.0$ and the $MS_{wg} = 3.0$. $F =$ _____.

32/3 = 10.67

252. Consulting an *F* table (as you will shortly learn to do) gives us the information that we would expect *F*, in these circumstances and when H_0 is true, to reach or exceed 5.99 less than 5 percent of the time. Since our observed *F* is 10.67, we beat the critical *F* from the table of 5.99 and so there is less than a 5 percent chance that the H_0 is (true, false). _____

True

253. With the likelihood of the H_0 being true falling below .05 percent, many researchers would reject H_0. They thus would accept the belief that there (was, was not) a Ritalin effect. _____

Was

254. Other, more conservative researchers might not wish to reject H_0 unless its likelihood fell below .01 percent (or an even smaller value). A table lets us know that, even when H_0 is true, *F* can by chance get as large as 13.75 with samples of the size we used. The 10.67 that we got fails to equal or beat this critical value. It falls within the range that we would expect by chance. The likelihood that H_0 is true is thus (greater than, the same as, less than) 1 percent. _____

Greater Than

255. This 5 percent and 1 percent are called the **levels of significance.** In our example, if we had used the 5 percent level of significance, we would (reject, retain) H_0. _____ At the 1 percent level of significance, we would (reject, retain) H_0. _____.

Reject
Retain

256. Since there is less than a 5 percent chance that we are wrong in rejecting the H_0, we are over 95 percent confident that a Ritalin effect is pre-

sent. Can we be over 99 percent confident of a Ritalin effect?
_____

No, because we failed to equal or beat the critical F of 13.75 for 5 percent.

257. The greater the variation between groups as compared with the variation within groups, the greater will be the size of the _____ ratio.

$\overline{F}$

258. Pictured below are two different experiments, one by Dr. Abel (experiment A) and one by Dr. Baker (experiment B). Both experiments compared the results of three different methods for teaching reading. In both experiments the means for the three conditions were 3, 4, and 5, respectively. The results **within** any one condition varied less in experiment A than in experiment B. Experiment A showed significant results, while experiment B did not. To see why, note that each of the groups in Dr. Abel's experiment was less variable (and thus her experiment had a smaller within variance) than those in Dr. Baker's experiment. Since the means were the same in each experiment, the **between variance** would be the same, assuming the number of subjects were the same in experiments A and B. The F ratio (or the **between variance** divided by the **within variance**) would thus be larger in the experiment by Dr. _____ .

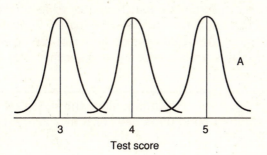

Test score

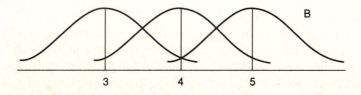

Abel

259. The size of F required for significance (the critical F), varies by the number of groups, the number of subjects in each group, and the amount of confidence with which the researcher wishes to speak. Would the F required for the .01 level be higher or lower than that for the .05 level? _____

Higher

260. The critical F required for significance with particular sample sizes, numbers of groups, and confidence levels is found in Appendix A. (A brief example may be found in Table 4 following Frame 273.) An F value of one or less is always nonsignificant. Thus, if this were the case, it (would, would not) be necessary to consult an F table. _____

Would Not

ANOVA: Practical Computations

261. Suppose that the visual perception tests had been given under differ-ent conditions to different children, the matching of child to condition being random. The researcher might now ask whether the treatments really made a difference. If the researcher decides that the different conditions probably did make a difference, she is (rejecting, retaining) the null hypothesis (H_0). _____

Rejecting, since the H_0 is that the different conditions have exactly a zero effect.

262. The assignment of treatments might have run something like this: Don and Ray were warned of dire consequences if they do badly on the test; Jan, May, and Joy make up a sample that received neither warn-ing nor encouragement; Jim, Sam, Fay, and Art were told only that they would probably do very well.

The visual perception data, grouped by treatment, would now look like this:

Warned Subjects	Scores	Neutral Subjects	Scores	Encouraged Subjects	Scores
Don	0	Jan	2	Jim	4
Ray	4	May	4	Sam	4
		Joy	6	Fay	6
				Art	6

Even though it is generally desirable to have the number of subjects in each treatment group be as near to equal as is convenient, notice that equality is not necessary.

As review, ignore the division into treatment groups and compute the SS for all nine scores. _____ What is the df? _____ Remember that

$$SS_{total} = \Sigma X^2 - \frac{(\Sigma X)^2}{N}$$

$$= 176 - \frac{36^2}{9}$$

$$= 32.$$

$SS_{total} = 32$
df $= N - 1 = 9 - 1 = 8$

For the problem that you do, assume that Ima and Lil receive one treatment, while Dot, Hal, and Sue receive the other. The breakdown would now be:

Treatment A		Treatment B	
Ima	0	Dot	2
Lil	2	Hal	3
		Sue	8

263. As further review, compute the SS and df for the **total** sample of five scores. $SS_{total} =$ _____ . $df_{total} =$ _____ .

$SS_{total} = 32$
$df_{total} = N - 1 = 5 - 1 = 4$

264. Because different **subjects** get different treatments, this is called a **between subjects design.** If each subject were measured on different levels of treatment, it would be a **within subjects design.**

If we had 80 subjects divided into two treatment groups of 40 each, it would be a _____ subjects design. If the 80 subjects were measured before and after, it would be a _____ subjects design.

Between
Within

265. You will learn how to do a one-way, between subjects ANOVA. The **total SS** is composed of the **SS between groups** and the SS within groups (which is also called the **SS error**).

Since the total SS has been calculated, it is necessary only to calculate the SS between groups. If $SS_{total} = SS_{bg} + SS_{wg}$, how could we get the SS_{wg} if we already had the SS_{total} and the SS_{bg}? _____

Subtraction ($SS_{wg} = SS_{total} - SS_{bg}$)

266. **Computing the SS_{bg}**
Sum up all scores in a cell, square this total, and divide by the number of scores in the cell. Total this value for all cells, and then subtract the CF. The result is the SS between groups (SS_{bg}).

I Did This	You Try This

$$SS_{bg} = \frac{(\Sigma X_1)^2}{n_1} + \frac{(\Sigma X_2)^2}{n_2} + \ldots - CF$$

$$\frac{(\Sigma X_1)^2}{n_1} = \frac{(0 + 4)^2}{2} = 8$$

$$\frac{(\Sigma X_1)^2}{n_2} = \frac{(2 + 4 + 6)^2}{3} = 48$$

$$\frac{(\Sigma X_3)^2}{n_3} = \frac{(4 + 4 + 6 + 6)^2}{4} = 100$$

$$CF = \frac{(\Sigma X_{ALL})^2}{N_{ALL}} = \frac{36^2}{9} = 144$$

$$SS_{bg} = 8 + 48 + 100 - 144 = 12$$

$$SS_{bg} = _____$$

13.33

267. With k equal to the number of groups, the df between groups (df_{bg}) is equal to $k - 1$.

I Did This	You Try This
$df_{bg} = k - 1$	
$\quad = 3 - 1$	
$\quad = 2$	$df_{bg} = $ _____
	1

268. The SS within groups (SS_{wg}) is equal to the total SS (SS_{total}) minus the SS between groups (SS_{bg}).

I Did This	You Try This
$SS_{wg} = SS_{total} - SS_{bg}$	
$\quad = 32 - 12$	
$\quad = 20$	$SS_{wg} = $ _____
	36 – 13.33 = 22.67

269. Similarly, the degrees of freedom within groups (df_{wg}) is equal to the total df (df_{total}) minus the df between groups (df_{bg}).

I Did This	You Try This
$df_{wg} = df_{total} - df_{bg}$	
$\quad = 8 - 2$	
$\quad = 6$	$df_{wg} = $ _____
	3

270. For each of the components of the total variance, the estimate of variance or **mean square** (MS) is equal to the SS divided by the df.

I Did This	You Try This
$MS_{bg} = SS_{bg} / df_{bg}$	
$\quad = 12/2$	
$\quad = 6$	$MS_{bg} = $ _____
	13.33/1 = 13.33

$MS_{wg} = SS_{wg} / df_{wg}$	
$\quad = 20/6$	
$\quad = 3.33$	$MS_{wg} = $ _____
	22.67/3 = 7.56

271. For F divide MS_{bg} by MS_{wg}

	I Did This	You Try This
	$F = MS_{bg}/MS_{wg}$	
	$= 6/3.33$	
	$= 1.80$	$F = $ _____

13.33/7.56 = 1.76

272. From all the completed work, the finished table for **my** problem looks like this:

	SS	df		MS
F				
Total	32	8		
Between	12	2	6.0	1.8
Within	20	6	3.2	

You fill in the table for the problem **you** did.

	SS	df		MS
F				
Total	____	____		
Between	____	____	____	____
Within	____	____	____	

	SS	df	MS	F
Total	**36.00**	**4**		
Between	**13.33**	**1**	**13.33**	**1.76**
Within	**22.67**	**3**	**7.56**	

273. The calculated F can now be compared with the values in a table showing F values that cut off the most extreme upper 5 percent of the chance distribution (see Table 4). To use this table, follow across the top until the column for the df between groups is reached. For the problem I did, $df_{bg} = 2$. Then follow the left-hand column down to the df within groups (df error). For my problem, $df_{wg} = 6$. The table value is

_____ .

5.14

Table 4   .05 Critical Values for the Distribution of *F*

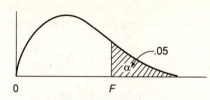

Degrees of freedom within groups	Degrees of freedom between groups		
	1	2	3
1	161.4	199.5	215.7
2	18.51	19.0	19.16
3	10.13	9.55	9.28
4	7.71	6.94	6.59
5	6.61	5.79	5.41
6	5.99	5.14	4.76
8	5.32	4.46	4.07
20	4.35	3.49	3.10
30	4.17	3.32	2.92
40	4.08	3.23	2.84
60	4.00	3.15	2.76
120	3.92	3.07	2.68
α	3.84	2.99	2.60

274. For us to reject the null hypothesis (that no differences exist among the means), our calculated *F* would have to equal or exceed (meet or beat) this **critical** table value. Since our 1.33 does not meet or beat 5.14, we retain the null hypothesis. We would report, "No significant difference (at the .05 level) was detected among the means."

For the problem you did, **calculated** *F* was _____, df_{bg} was _____, df_{wg} was _____ and the critical *F* is _____.

1.76	**1**
3	**10.13**

275. Since our calculated *F* (fails to, does) _____ meet or beat the table *F*, our decision follows that we (do not have evidence to, may) _____ reject the null hypothesis and conclude that (no evidence was found to suggest, it is most probable) _____ that the treatments make a difference in the population.

_____

Fails To
Do Not Have Evidence to
No Evidence Was Found to Suggest

276. When only two means are being compared, a technique called the *t* test has been much used. It involves more computation than analysis of variance and offers little in the way of advantages. If computation of a *t* between two independent means is called for, just compute *F* and take its square root. When two groups are being compared, *t* = square root of *F*. If $F = 9$ then $t =$ _____.

_____
3

277. *F* tests and *t* tests deal with sample means and are based on the assumption that the distribution of the variables compared is pretty much normal (i.e., approximates a normal curve). Is it reasonable to assume that such values as achievement test scores, IQs, heights, weights, and the like, will be close to normally distributed? _____ Would this assumption always be correct? _____

_____
Yes
No

Computer Quick Start
_____
Computer entries in normal font
Output in bold normal font
Comments in bold italics font
For more help, see Appendix C

Analysis of Variance (ANOVA) (ONEWAY) using MINITAB

Data File demo.dat	Program File anov_mtb.pgm	Program File Comments
0 1 6 0	READ 'demo.dat' C1 C2 C3 C4	*C2 and C3 are not used. A*
2 1 4 0	NAME C1 'x' C4 'group'	*slightly advanced way to read*
2 2 3 1	ONEWAY C1 C4	*in data would have allowed*
3 3 2 1		*us to read in only the first and*
8 7 0 1		*fourth columns. The second*
		column in the ONEWAY
		statement is the indicator
		variable that shows which
		group the scores are in.

COMPUTER OUTPUT (IN PART)

MTB > EXEC 'anov_mtb.pgm'
Executing from file: anovamtb.pgm
Entering data from file: demo.dat
5 rows read.
ANALYSIS OF VARIANCE ON x

SOURCE	DF	SS	MS	F	p
group	1	13.33	13.33	1.76	0.276
ERROR	3	22.67	7.56		
TOTAL	4	36.00			

INDIVIDUAL 95% CI'S FOR MEAN
BASED ON POOLED STDEV

LEVEL	N	MEAN	STDEV	---+---------+---------+---------+---
0	2	1.000	1.414	(----------------*---------------)
1	3	4.333	3.215	(-------------*------------)

---+---------+---------+---------+---
POOLED STDEV = 2.749   −4.0   0.0   4.0   8.0

Comments:

The p of .276 reported above is consistent with our finding in Frame 263 that the probability of finding an F this large if there was no difference in the population is > .05 and thus the differences were not significant at the .05 level. The pooled standard deviation is the square root of the MS for error (or MS_{wg}).

Analysis of Variance (ANOVA) using SAS

Data File demo.dat	Program File anovasas.pgm	Program File Comments
0 1 6 0	DATA;	*DATA; enables advanced file*
2 1 4 0	INFILE 'demo.dat';	*handling beyond this book.*
2 2 3 1	INPUT x y z group;	*Enter line as is. Remember ; at*
3 3 2 1	PROC ANOVA;	*end of lines. The variables, y*
8 7 0 1	CLASS group;	*and z, are not used. A slightly*
	MODEL x = group;	*more advanced way to read in*
	RUN;	*data would have allowed us to*
		read in only X and group.
		CLASS group; tells SAS the
		numbers in group are to be
		treated as nominal.

COMPUTER OUTPUT (IN PART)

The SAS System
Analysis of Variance Procedure

Dependent Variable: X

Source	DF	Sum of Squares	Mean Square	F Value	Pr > F
Model	1	13.33333333	13.33333333	1.76	0.2761
Error	3	22.66666667	7.55555556		
Corrected Total	4	36.00000000			

	R-Square	C.V.	Root MSE	X Mean
	0.370370	91.62457	2.748737	3.000000

Comments:

R-SQUARE is, in this simple case, r^2 which is the proportion of the variance of the dependent variable (x) that can be predicted from the independent variable (group). It can also be computed as SS_{bg}/SS_{total}. The SS_{bg} is the same as the SS model. Thus 13.33333333/36 = .370370 which checks with our earlier finding that the correlation between x and group was .609 (the square root of .370370).

The C.V. is 100 times the standard deviation of the dependent variable (x) divided by its mean giving a measure of variability free of arbitrary units. The standard deviation used here is the Root MSE, which is simply the square root of the Error Mean Square.

ANOVA (ONEWAY)using SPSS

Data File demo.dat	Program File anov_sps.sps	Program File Comments
0 1 6 0	DATA LIST	**DATA LIST starts the data**
2 1 4 0	File= 'demo.dat'	**input. The FILE= line gives**
2 2 3 1	FREE/ x y z group.	**the file containing the data.**
3 3 2 1	ONEWAY x BY group.	**FREE/ allows data to be**
8 7 0 1	/STATISTICS= ALL.	**read in free form.**

Leave a blank at start of all lines except first of a command and notice . at end of command.

COMPUTER OUTPUT (IN PART)

- - - - - O N E W A Y - - - - -

Variable X
By Variable GROUP

Analysis of Variance

Source	D.F.	Sum of Squares	Mean Squares	F Ratio	F Prob.
Between Groups	1	13.3333	13.3333	1.7647	.2761
Within Groups	3	22.6667	7.5556		
Total	4	36.0000			

Group	Count	Mean	Standard Deviation	Standard Error	95 Pct Conf Int for Mean
Grp 0	2	1.0000	1.4142	1.0000	−11.7062 TO 13.7062
Grp 1	3	4.3333	3.2146	1.8559	−3.6521 TO 12.3188
Total	5	3.0000	3.0000	1.3416	−.7249 TO 6.7249

Comments:

The F Ratio of 1.7647 matches the 1.76 you got in frame 271. The F Prob. at .2761 squares with our conclusion that the probability of an F this large by chance is >.05 and thus the difference in the means is not significant at the .05 level. The Standard Error for the Total of 1.3416 matches the 1.34 you obtained in Frame 165 and the 95 Pct Confidence Interval for the Mean ranging from −.7249 to 6.7249 is within rounding error of the −.73 and 6.73 you got in Frame 168.

OPEN BOOK QUIZ ON ANALYSIS OF VARIANCE (ANOVA)
(Answers on page 186)

1. ANOVA is used primarily to test the significance of differences between _____.

2. The total SS is made up of the between SS and the _____ SS. Assume an experiment with two conditions and two subjects per condition.

Conditions
b_1 b_2
  1   5
  3   7

Compute the following:
a. Within SS _____
b. F _____

3. Is the difference in means between the two conditions significant at the .05 level? _____

Chi-Square Frequencies: (Expected and Observed)

One-Way (One-Dimensional) Chi-Square

278. Consider the following question: Are more babies born in one season than another? To investigate this, we could start off by gathering some birth dates from a randomly selected sample. Let's suppose that we now have a total of **40** birth dates and that we have defined the seasons so that spring, summer, fall, and winter each has an equal number of days expected ratio is thus 1 : 1 : 1. How many births out of the 40 would you **expect** in each season if, in fact, season did not make a difference?

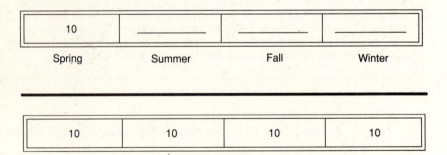

| 10 | _____ | _____ | _____ |
| Spring | Summer | Fall | Winter |

| 10 | 10 | 10 | 10 |

That is, the 40 birth dates would be evenly distributed among seasons.

279. When we group the **observed** birth dates of the 40 persons, they might distribute like this:

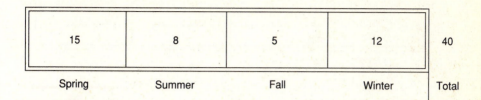

Spring	Summer	Fall	Winter	Total
15	8	5	12	40

The question now would be "Is the fact that the observed birth dates are different from what we expected more likely due to chance, or does it more likely represent actual population differences in birth rate during the different seasons?" To decide this question of whether frequencies are significantly different than expected, a very popular, easy, and useful test is the **chi-square test.**

To perform the chi-square test, summarize the information below, with E in the small box for each cell. This is the traditional format. Later, we will use a more modern format that is better suited to computer output.

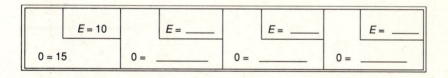

$E = 10$	$E = $ _____	$E = $ _____	$E = $ _____
$O = 15$	$O = $ _____	$O = $ _____	$O = $ _____

10	10	10	10
15	8	5	12

280. Separately for each cell, subtract the expected frequency (E) from the observed frequency (O).

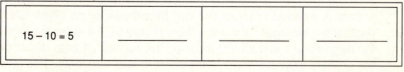

15 − 10 = 5	_____	_____	_____

$O - E$

-2   -5   2

281. Square these differences.

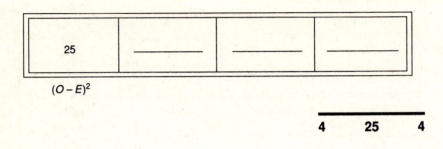

| 25 | ——— | ——— | ——— |

$(O - E)^2$

4   25   4

282. Divide each of these squared differences by E.

| $\dfrac{25}{10}$ = 2.5 | ——— | ——— | ——— |

$(O - E)^2/E$

.4   2.5   .4

283. Add all of these up. The result is chi-square (χ^2). _____

2.5 + .4 + 2.5 + .4 = 5.8

284. A relatively large chi-square may indicate that the Es differed more from the Os than is likely by chance. As to how large a value for chi-square is needed to reject the null hypothesis of no difference in the population, we again consult a table (Table 5). To enter the table, find the degrees of freedom (df) by using the number of cells minus one. In the present case we have four cells (the four seasons). The df will be

_____.

4 − 1 = 3

Table 5   .05 Points for the Distribution of Chi-Square

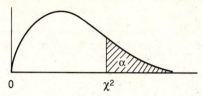

0   χ^2

(For a more complete table, see Appendix A, Table E, page 166.)

Degrees of Freedom	Chi-Square
1	3.84
2	5.99
3	**7.81**
4	9.49
6	12.59
8	15.51
12	21.03
20	31.41
30	43.77
60	79.08
120	146.57

285. For this problem, what value of chi-square would we have to meet or beat to declare that a significant (.05 level) difference exists between what we would expect if there were no population difference and what we have observed? _____

7.81

286. Since our computed chi-square of 5.80 fails to meet or beat 7.81, we may now (reject, retain) the hypothesis that only chance has caused any differences between expected frequencies and observed frequencies. _____

Retain

287. Retaining H_0 is not the same as saying that we proved there is no difference. Consider the way that many people feel about elves. These people find no evidence that elves exist, but, on the other hand, they have failed to prove the nonexistence of elves. Even if you peered un-

der a million mushrooms, an elf could be sitting beneath the very next one. In this analogy, the H_0 is the (existence of elves, the nonexistence of elves). _____

The Nonexistence of Elves

Two-Way (Two-Dimensional) Chi-Square

288. Chi-square analysis can also be used to find out whether there is a relationship between how subjects fall into different categories. Chi-square analysis can show whether there is a probable relationship between ethnic group and voting, income and type of car driven, gender and color preference, educational level and type of music preferred, and so on.

As an example, assume a six-room house where only men were allowed in three rooms and only women in the other three. Different drinks were served in each set of rooms, so the house plan would look like the figure shown here.

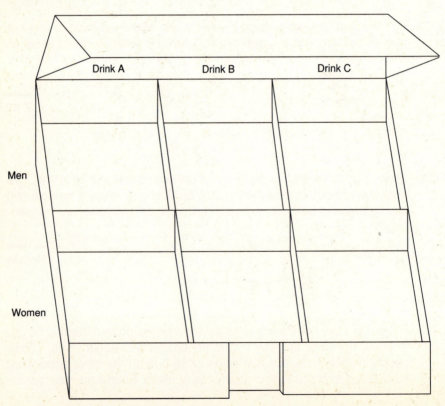

After a large party gets going, we gently lift the roof off the house and we see what is illustrated in the figure shown here.

Observe the frequency in each category (room). What is the observed frequency (*O*) in each category?

	Drink A	Drink B	Drink C
Men	_____	_____	_____
Women	_____	_____	_____

	Drink A	Drink B	Drink C
Men	10	5	15
Women	5	10	5

289. Is there some relationship between gender and drink preferred? It seems that women might tend toward drink B and men toward drink C, but chance could cause some effect in our sample even if there were no relationship in the population.

It is the null hypothesis approach again. We first hypothesize that there is no relationship between gender and drink preferred. If there were no relationship, given that 30 out of the 50 people are men (60 percent), what percent of those preferring Drink C would you expect to be men? _____

60 Percent

290. Since 20 people preferred Drink C and you would expect 60 percent of them to be men, what would be the expected frequency (E) for men preferring Drink C? _____ .

60 Percent of 20 = 12

291. We can summarize the separate effects by totaling around the margins. These totals are called **marginals.** Complete the marginals for the table in Frame 288.

	Drink A	Drink B	Drink C	
Men	10	5	15	_____
Women	5	10	5	_____
	_____	_____	_____	

			30
			20
15	15	20	

292. The sum of the expected frequencies in one column (or line) also equals the marginal. Since 20 people prefer Drink C and the E for men is 12, the E for women for Drink C must be _____.

20 − 12 = 8

293. In case this intuitive approach to getting expected frequencies isn't clear, an alternative formula may help:

$$E \text{ for any square} = \frac{(\text{Column marginal})(\text{Row marginal})}{\text{Grand total for all cells}}.$$

For the present example: E for men, Drink A:

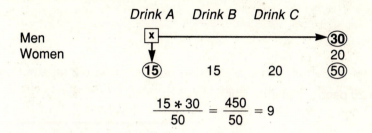

	Drink A	Drink B	Drink C	
Men	x		30	
Women	15	15	20	20 / 50

$$\frac{15 * 30}{50} = \frac{450}{50} = 9$$

Compute E for remaining cells, and complete this table.

$O = 10$ $E = 9$	$O = 5$ $E =$ _____	$O = 15$ $E =$ _____	30
$O = 5$ $E =$ _____	$O = 10$ $E =$ _____	$O = 5$ $E =$ _____	20
15	15	20	50

$O = 10$ $E = 9$	$O = 5$ $E = 9$	$O = 15$ $E = 12$	30
$O = 5$ $E = 6$	$O = 10$ $E = 6$	$O = 5$ $E = 8$	20
15	15	20	50

294. Knowing O and E for each cell, we make the final calculations. For each separate cell, compute $(O - E)^2/E$.

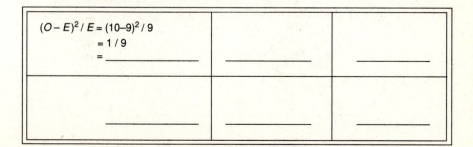

$(O - E)^2 / E = (10-9)^2 / 9$ $= 1/9$ $=$ _____	_____	_____
_____	_____	_____

	Drink A	Drink B	Drink C
Men	0.111	1.778	0.750
Women	0.167	2.667	1.125

295. The sum of $(O - E)^2/E$ for all of these cells is called **chi-square.** For the present problem, chi-square $(\chi^2) = 0.111 + 1.778 + 0.75 + 0.167$ + _____ + _____ = _____.

2.667   1.125   6.598

296. If the observed frequencies were quite different from the expected frequencies, we would find each $(O - E)^2$ and thus

$$\chi^2 = \Sigma \frac{(O - E)^2}{E}$$

to be relatively (small, large). _____

Large

Significance Testing of Chi-Square

297. To enter the chi-square table in doing a two-dimensional chi-square analysis, find the degrees of freedom by multiplying the number of rows minus 1 by the number of columns minus 1. In this case it is $(2 - 1) * (3 - 1) = 2$.

If you are better at coloring than arithmetic, color in the bottom row and the right column. Count the number of cells left. For example, what is the df?

We can color in the following:

Four cells are left, so the df = 4.
Now you do this one either way you want. What is the df?

8

298. In the present problem (the gender-drink study), what value of chi-square would we have to meet or beat to declare a significant (.05 level) relationship between gender and preferred drink? _____

5.99

299. Since our computed chi-square of 6.598 beats the critical value of 5.99, at the .05 level we (reject, retain) _____ the null hypothesis of no relationship and (accept, reject) _____ the alternate hypothesis.

Reject
Accept

300. Two final points about chi-square: If there is only one degree of freedom, a special adjustment (subtracting .5 from the absolute value of

$O - E$ before squaring) is generally applied. This is called the **correction for continuity.**

Give df for each of the designs below.
A._____ B._____ C._____ D._____
For which designs would the correction for continuity be absolutely required? _____ _____

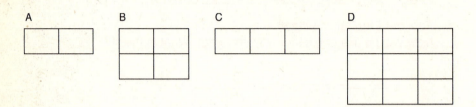

1	1	2	4

A and B (Each Has Just 1 df)

301. Chi-square probabilities are not very accurate unless at least 80 percent of the expected values exceed 5. If **observed** data of 46 FOR and 4 AGAINST had an expected ratio of 1 : 1, could a chi-square analysis be appropriate? _____

**Yes, It Is the Expected,
Not the Observed, That Counts.
The Expected Were 25 25**

302. In the two sets of results shown below, the observed frequencies are given. Assume an expected ratio of 1 : 1. Fill in the E, the $O - E$ and the df for each table.

Table A	FOR	AGAINST	Total df = _____
	$O = 10$	$O = 20$	30
	$E = $_____	$E = $_____	
	$O - E = $_____	$O - E = $_____	

Table B	FOR	AGAINST	Total	df = _____
Women	$O =$ 10 $E =$ _____ $O - E =$ _____	$O =$ 30 $E =$ _____ $O - E =$ _____	40	
Men	$O =$ 20 $E =$ _____ $O - E =$ _____	$O =$ 20 $E =$ _____ $O - E =$ _____	40	
Total	30	50	80	

Table A	FOR	AGAINST	Total df = 1
	$O =$ 10 $E =$ 15 $O - E =$ -5	$O =$ 20 $E =$ 15 $O - E =$ 5	30

Table B	FOR	AGAINST	Total df = 1
Women	$O =$ 10 $E =$ 15 $O - E =$ -5	$O =$ 30 $E =$ 25 $O - E =$ 5	40
Men	$O =$ 20 $E =$ 15 $O - E =$ 5	$O =$ 20 $E =$ 25 $O - E =$ -5	40
Total	30	50	80

303. Since the df for each study was 1, we need to make the correction above of taking .5 from the absolute value for each $O - E$ before squaring. For the first cell (the FOR cases in the one-way table), $O - E$ $= 10 - 15 = -5$. Absolute means calling a value positive whether it is negative or positive. The symbol is to include the value inside two upright lines. Absolute value for $10 - 15 = |10 - 15| = |-5| = +5$. For each cell compute $|O - E|$, $|O - E| - .5$, $(|O - E| - .5)^2$ and $(|O - E| - .5)^2/E$.

Table A	FOR		AGAINST	
$\|O - E\|$	= 5	$\|O - E\|$	= _____
$\|O - E\| - .5$	= 4.5	$\|O - E\| - .5$	= _____
$(\|O - E\| - .5)^2$	= 20.25	$(\|O - E\| - .5)^2$	= _____
$(\|O - E\| - .5)^2/15$	= 1.35	$(\|O - E\| - .5)^2/15$	= _____

Table A	FOR		AGAINST	
	$\|O-E\|$	= 5	$\|O-E\|$	= 5
	$\|O-E\|-.5$	= 4.5	$\|O-E\|-.5$	= 4.5
	$(\|O-E\|-.5)^2$	= 20.25	$(\|O-E\|-.5)^2$	= 20.25
	$(\|O-E\|-.5)^2/15$	= 1.35	$(\|O-E\|-.5)^2/15$	= 1.35

Table B	FOR		AGAINST	
Women	$\|O-E\|$	= 5	$\|O-E\|$	= _____
	$\|O-E\|-.5$	= 4.5	$\|O-E\|-.5$	= _____
	$(\|O-E\|-.5)^2$	= 20.25	$(\|O-E\|-.5)^2$	= _____
	$(\|O-E\|-.5)^2/15$	= 1.35	$(\|O-E\|-.5)^2/25$	= _____
Men	$\|O-E\|$	= _____	$\|O-E\|$	= _____
	$\|O-E\|-.5$	= _____	$\|O-E\|-.5$	= _____
	$(\|O-E\|-.5)^2$	= _____	$(\|O-E\|-.5)^2$	= _____
	$(\|O-E\|-.5)^2/15$	= _____	$(\|O-E\|-.5)^2/25$	= _____

Table B	FOR		AGAINST	
Women	$\|O-E\|$	= 5	$\|O-E\|$	= 5
	$\|O-E\|-.5$	= 4.5	$\|O-E\|-.5$	= 4.5
	$(\|O-E\|-.5)^2$	= 20.25	$(\|O-E\|-.5)^2$	= 20.25
	$(\|O-E\|-.5)^2/15$	= 1.35	$(\|O-E\|-.5)^2/25$	= 0.81
Men	$\|O-E\|$	= 5	$\|O-E\|$	= 5
	$\|O-E\|-.5$	= 4.5	$\|O-E\|-.5$	= 4.5
	$(\|O-E\|-.5)^2$	= 20.25	$(\|O-E\|-.5)^2$	= 20.25
	$(\|O-E\|-.5)^2/15$	= 1.35	$(\|O-E\|-.5)^2/25$	= 0.81

304. This correction is called the **Yates correction for continuity** or some part of that name, such as Yates correction or correction for continuity. With $(\|O-E\|-.5)^2/E$ computed for each cell, we add these, giving the corrected chi-square. The entire formula for chi-square with the Yates correction for continuity now reads as follows:

$$\chi^2 = \Sigma \frac{(\|O-E\|-.5)^2}{E}$$

The corrected chi-square for A = _____, for B = _____.

2.700
4.320

305. For the first chi-square we found of 2.700, we can go directly to the chi-square table in Appendix A. There we see that to reject H_0 at the .05 level for 1 df, our chi-square has to beat or at least equal the critical value of 3.841 (which it does, does not). How about table B? Significant at .05? _____ Significant at .01? _____

> **2.700 does not meet or beat**
> **the critical value of 3.841.**
> **Yes. 4.320 beats 3.841.**
> **No. 4.320 does not meet or beat 6.635.**

Computer Quick Start

Computer entries in normal font
Output in bold normal font
Comments in bold italics font
For more help, see Appendix C

Chi-Square using MINITAB

Neither data nor program files were needed.
Output follows directly after input.

MTB > READ c1 c2 c3
DATA > 10 5 15
DATA > 5 10 5
DATA > END
2 rows read.
MTB > NAME C1 'drink_a' C2 'drink_b' C3 'drink_c'
MTB > CHISQUARE C1 C2 C3
Expected counts are printed below observed counts

	drink_a	drink_b	drink_c	Total
1	10	5	15	30
	9.00	9.00	12.00	
2	5	10	5	20
	6.00	6.00	8.00	
Total	15	15	20	50

ChiSq = 0.111 + 1.778 + 0.750 + 0.167 + 2.667 + 1.125 = 6.597

df = 2
MTB > CDF 6.597;
SUBC> CHISQUARE 2.
      6.5970   0.9631
MTB > LET K1 = 1 − .9631
MTB > PRINT K1

K1   0.0369000
MTB > STOP

Comments:

This Quick Start is different from the others in this book in that it is interactive. There are so few data to be read when we already know the cell totals that interactive is probably the way to go.
The data are from Frame 293.
After we have signed on to MINITAB, we instruct it to read in 3 columns. It then gives us the DATA> prompt, and we enter the columns of data. When done entering data, type END. The NAME C1 etc. line is optional. Note the single quotes around names.
The chi-square of 6.597 is what we got in Frame 297.
MINITAB does not easily give P values for chi-square nor does it seem to do Fisher's Exact Test. If MINITAB is all you have, it would probably pay to do chi-square problems with 1 df by calculator.
We can get a P value by the rather awkward last 4 lines. CDF stands for the cumulative density function which is 1−P. After we entered CDF 6.597; (don't forget the ;), we typed CHISQUARE 2. (don't forget the .) where 2 was the df. MINITAB then gives 1−P.

Chi-Square using SAS

No Data File Used	Program File *chi_sas.pgm*	Program File Comments

	DATA;
	INPUT gender $ drink $ count;
	LINES;
	   men A 10
	   men B 5
	   men C 15
	women A 5
	women B 10
	women C 5
	RUN;
	PROC FREQ;
	TABLES gender*drink /EXACT;
	WEIGHT count;
	RUN;
		DATA; enables advanced file handling beyond this book. Enter as is. Remember ; at end of lines. LINES; is followed by data that are just like they would be for an external file. So little data are needed if we already have frequencies that they can be read in directly. The $ after gender and drink signals an alphabetical variable. It was an easy way here of labeling the levels. TABLES gender*drink calls for the cross-tabulation. The /EXACT calls for a test called Fisher's Exact Test (commented on below). Weight count; says use count as a total for a cell rather than just as a score.

COMPUTER OUTPUT (IN PART) SAS

TABLE OF GENDER BY DRINK

GENDER Frequency Percent Row Pct Col Pct	DRINK A	B	C	Total
men	10 20.00 33.33 66.67	5 10.00 16.67 33.33	15 30.00 50.00 75.00	30 60.00
women	5 10.00 25.00 33.33	10 20.00 50.00 66.67	5 10.00 25.00 25.00	20 40.00
Total	15 30.00	15 30.00	20 40.00	50 100.00

STATISTICS FOR TABLE OF GENDER BY DRINK

Statistic	DF	Value	Prob
Chi-Square	2	6.597	0.037
Fisher's Exact Test (2-Tail)			0.045
Sample Size = 50			

Comments:

Fisher's Exact Test is generally done only on computers because it involves many computations. It is to be preferred over the chi-square test when it is available. We read the probability (Prob) directly. Since it is 0.045, the differences are significant at the .05 level but not at the .01 level.
The Prob using a Chi-Square of 0.037 is consistent with our computations by hand in which we concluded that chi-square was significant at the .05 level but not at the .01 level. That is, if only chance were involved, the probability, given the marginals we got, of a chi-square this large is 0.037, more rare than .05 but not as rare as .01.

Chi-Square using SPSS

No Data File Used	Program File chi_sps.sps	Program File Comments

```
           DATA LIST
             FREE/ gender (A5) drink (A) count
             WEIGHT BY count.
           BEGIN DATA
              Men  A 10
              Men  B  5
              Men  C 15
           Women  A  5
           Women  B 10
           Women  C  5
           END DATA.
           CROSSTABS TABLES= gender BY drink
             /STATS= CHISQ.
```

BEGIN DATA is followed by data that are just like they would be for an external file. So little data are needed if we already have frequencies that they can be read in directly. The A5 and A after gender and drink signal alphabetical variables and their length, an easy way to label levels. WEIGHT BY count. says use count as the cell total rather than only as a score.

COMPUTER OUTPUT (IN PART) SPSS

GENDER by DRINK

Count	DRINK			
GENDER	A	B	C	Row Total
Men	10	5	15	30 / 60.0
Women	5	10	5	20 / 40.0
Column Total	15 / 30.0	15 / 30.0	20 / 40.0	50 / 100.0

Chi-Square	Value	DF	Significance
Pearson	6.59722	2	0.03693

Comments:

The full name for the regular chi-square is the Pearson Chi-Square and thus "Pearson" in the output above. The value of 6.59722 checks within rounding error with the 6.598 found in Frame 269. The P of .03693 checks with our conclusion that the probability of observed frequencies differing this much by chance from what we expected is less than .05 or 5%. Chi-square is thus significant at the .05 level. It is not significant at the .01 level however since .0393 is greater than .01 or 1%.

Had we included the program (or SYNTAX) line STATS= ALL. we would have witnessed an impressive demonstration of the diversity of tests that can be performed on tables. Since these tests are not covered in our brief book, that output was not shown.

A weakness of SPSS is that it only does Fisher's Exact Test (see comments on SAS output just above) if it has an expected frequency of less than 5. SPSS is smart enough, however, to perform the Yate's Correction for Continuity for all 2 by 2 tables.

OPEN BOOK QUIZ ON CHI-SQUARE
(Answers start on page 187)

1. To find out whether means differ significantly from each other, use
_____, but to find out whether frequencies differ from the ex-
pected, we used _____.

2. A sample of 30 voters was asked which of three candidates they
planned to vote for, with the following results:

Candidate	Frequency
Smith	5
Jones	20
Baker	4

Test the hypothesis that, in the population, there is no difference in
preference for any of the candidates. Conclusion? _____

3. A sample of children and adults was asked their preference on car
size and the results were:

	Compact	Medium	Full
Children	20	30	10
Adults	10	20	30

If there is no difference between the preference pattern of children
and adults in the population, what frequency would you expect for
children preferring compact cars? _____

4. For Problem 3, compute chi-square. _____

5. For Problem 3, what chi-square would be needed for significance at
the .05 level? _____

Measurement

Scores

Raw Scores

306. The number of correct answers that a person gets on a test is the **raw score**. Assuming that each question on a test counted one point, a raw score of 12 would mean that an individual answered _____ questions correctly.

‾‾

12

307. The raw score alone is a poor indicator of test performance. For example, a raw score of 12 points out of a possible total of 12 points suggests good performance. A raw score of 12 points out of a possible total of 60 points suggests poor performance. In both cases, 12 points is the _____ _____.

Raw Score

308. A better indicator of test performance is the **percentage score** (the number of correct answers divided by the total number of questions multiplied by 100). What percentage score does 100 correct out of 400 questions receive? _____

25 Percent

309. Raw scores or percentage scores do not indicate a student's performance relative to the rest of the group. We cannot tell whether a percentage score of 91 percent is good or bad unless we know the other students' scores. It is possible that all the other students received scores higher than 91 percent. In such a case, 91 percent would be a low score _____ to the rest of the group.

Compared (or Relative)

Ranks

310. If scores are **ranked** from lowest to highest, we can indicate a person's position relative to the group by stating, for instance, that out of a group of ten, he ranks fourth from the bottom. What is the rank of the person with a test score of 91 percent in the distribution 83 percent, 85 percent, 88 percent, 91 percent, 96 percent? _____

Fourth (from the Bottom)

311. Although the sizes of the two hypothetical groups in the preceding frame were different (10 and 5), the selected individuals had the same _____.

   Just in passing, if you have ranks and wish to correlate them, there is a special easy formula (called **Spearman's Rank Order Correlation Coefficient**) but if you use the *r* that we learned (except using ranks) on a computer or calculator you will get exactly the same answer. Spearman's Rank Order Correlation is equivalent to the Pearson _____.

Rank
***r* or Product Moment Correlation Coefficient**

312. The person who ranked fourth in a group of ten was not as relatively high as the person who ranked fourth in a group of five. A rank by itself has little meaning unless the total number of people in the group is known. The weakness of ranks is that they depend upon the _____ of people in a group.

Number (or Total Number)

Percentile Ranks

313. The disadvantages of raw scores, percentage scores, and ranks are avoided by converting a person's rank to the number of cases she would equal or surpass if there were 100 cases in the group. Groups of

different sizes are more directly comparable by saying what a person's rank would be out of a group of _____.

100

314. If there were five people ranked 1 through 5, each person would represent 1/5 or 20 percent of the total group. The person with the rank of 4 would represent _____ percent of the group.

20

315. The three people ranking below the person with the rank of 4 would represent 3/5 or _____ percent of the group.

60

316. If we think of the person (or score) with the rank of 4 as being in the middle of the percentage the person represents, we could think of half of the 20 percent (or 10 percent) of the total group as having the same rank but exceeded by that particular person (or score) with the rank of 4. The person (or score) with the rank of 4 (out of 5) thus exceeds 60 percent by virtue of ranking above them and an additional 10 percent by virtue of being considered in the middle of those ranking the same. The total percent of scores the person exceeds is then _____ percent.

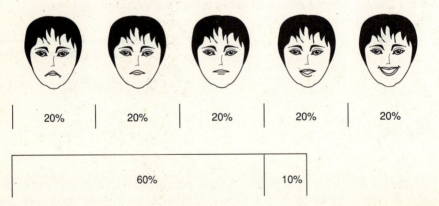

70

317. If there were ten scores ranked 1, 2, 3, 4, 5, 6, 7, 8, 9, 10, the score ranking 8 would exceed all scores ranking below it, which are _____ percent of the total group.

$$\overline{70}$$

318. Since the score ranking 8 may be thought of as exceeding half of the percentage it represents (i.e., ranking the same), it exceeds an additional half of 10 percent (or _____ percent). The total percentage that it exceeds is thus _____ percent + _____ percent = _____ percent.

$$\overline{5}$$
$$70 + 5 = 75$$

319. The **percentile rank (PR)** of a score is often defined as the percentage of scores having a lower rank plus one half the percentage of scores having the same rank. The score that ranked sixth out of 25 would have a PR = _____ + _____ = _____.

$$\overline{}$$
$$20 + 2 = 22$$

320. A convenient formula to use is:

$$PR = \frac{(N \text{ below the score}) + .5 \, (N \text{ at the score})}{\text{Total } N \text{ of the group}} * 100$$

Thus if one score ranked sixth out of 25,

$$PR = \frac{5 + (.5 * 1)}{25} * 100 = \frac{5.5}{25} * 100 = \underline{}.$$

$$\overline{22}$$

321. Compute the PR of the person with the test score of 91 in the distribution 83, 85, 91, 92, 95, 95, 95, 96, 97, 98. _____

$$\overline{25}$$

322. What is the PR of Bob's score?

Ann   77
Bob   81
Don   90
Nan   80
Ned   87
Pat   75
Sue   92

Don't forget to rank the scores.

———
50

Percentile Scores

323. Don't confuse percentile rank (PR) with percentile score. PR is the **cumulative percent** that a particular score occupies in a distribution (such as 50 in the preceding frame). The **percentile score** is the score that occupies the position of a particular cumulative percent. We have looked at one; the score that is 50 percent of the way through an ordered distribution is called the _____.

———————
Median Score

324. The percentile score follows the same principle as the median, but instead of being halfway through, is some percent through. The general name for the scores, some part through, is **quantiles.** Other popular quantiles in addition to the median (half through) are the **percentile** (some hundredths through), the **decile** (some tenth through), the **quintile** (some fifth through), and the **quartile.** Quartiles (Q1, Q2, or Q3) are some quarter through.

What quartile would be 75 percent through a distribution? _____
What percent of scores would be between Q1 and Q3? _____

What quartile is the same as the median? _____

**The Third Quartile or Q3 is three fourths through.
50 percent, Q1 is one fourth through, and Q3 is three
fourths through.
Q2**

325. In the distribution 20, 20, 20, 30, 40, 40, 60 the ranks of 30 and 60 are obviously 4 and 7, respectively, but the ranks of the tied scores 20 and by 40 are less obvious. The ranks occupied by 20 are 1, 2, and 3. The ranks occupied by 40 are _____ and _____.

5   6

326. When scores of the same value occupy more than one rank, the mean of those ranks is regarded as the tied-scores rank. For example, the rank of 20—that is, the mean of the ranks 1, 2, and 3—equals 2. The tied score 40, which occupies ranks 5 and 6, has a rank of _____.

5.5

327. The ranks for the whole distribution now run as follows:

Raw score:	20,	20,	20,	30,	40,	40,	60
Rank:	2,	2,	2,	4,	5.5,	5.5,	7

Did the calculations for tied ranks affect the ranks of untied scores? _____

No

Standard Scores (Revisited)

328. Since raw scores tend to cluster around the mean of a distribution, the percentile ranks do not have a constant relationship to the raw scores. From what is presented in the following percentile rank table, would it be possible to predict the omitted raw score? _____

Raw Score	Percentile Rank
10	5
22	10
23	15
28	20
?	25

No

329. Because percentile ranks do not have a constant relation to their scores, it is meaningless to average percentile ranks. Could you properly average the following percentile ranks: 2, 3, 5, 10? _____

No

330. A measure of relative standing that has a constant relationship to raw scores and that can be legitimately averaged is the standard score.

From what is presented in the following table, predict the omitted raw score. _____

Raw Score	Standard Score
40	-2
45	-1
50	0
55	+1
?	+2

60

Reliability and Validity

331. The statistical analogies in the following discussion are in parentheses.

A rifle placed in a vise might hit the same place consistently:

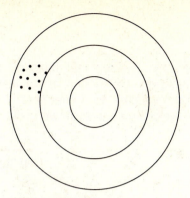

(This is reliability.)
In addition, the rifle might be on target:

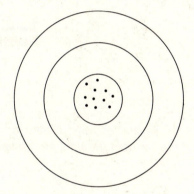

(This is validity.)
Could the rifle be on target (valid) if it weren't consistent (reliable)?

———————

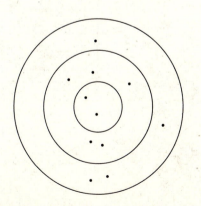

No

Reliability

332. **Reliability** is expressed as a correlation coefficient that measures the consistency of a test. If an instrument (test, experiment, or the like) is reliable, the same results should be obtainable time after time. If we were to use a very crude scale for weighing chemicals, we could not expect our results to be _____.

Reliable

333. Three common methods of measuring reliability are test-retest, equivalent forms, and split-half. If a test is to give consistent results, it has to be _____.

Reliable

334. **Test-retest reliability** is established by correlating the scores on the same test given at two different times. In the following illustration to measure test-retest reliability, would the form on the right be administered on May 1? _____

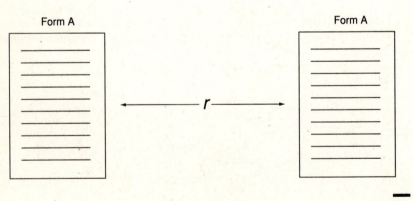

No

335. **Equivalent forms reliability** is established by the correlation between equivalent forms of the same test given at the same time. In the follow-

ing illustration to measure equivalent forms reliability, would the form on the right be administered on May 1? _____

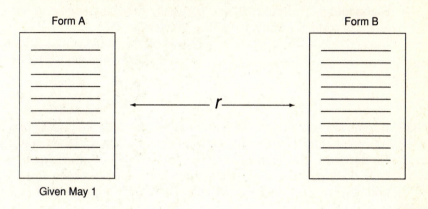

Form A   Form B

r

Given May 1

Yes

336. **Split-half reliability** is established by correlating the scores on two halves of the same test given at the same time. Split-half reliability measures internal consistency. If an entire test claims to measure paranoia, it should be true that the first half correlates highly with the second half. Variations on the same theme are: correlating the even items with the odd items or even pages with odd pages. All are focused on _____ _____.

Internal Consistency

337. A more sophisticated measure of internal consistency reliability, the computation of which is beyond this book, is **Chronbach's alpha.** It yields a composite value for each item correlated with all other items.

We have examined three criteria of reliability:
1. Stability
2. Equivalence
3. Internal consistency

Of these three criteria, Chronbach's alpha is a measure of _____.

Internal Consistency

338. With Chronbach's alpha, items can have any value such as: from 1 is low to 7 is high. If the items in a test are simply wrong or right (0 or 1), a simpler but equivalent form of Chronbach's alpha called the **Kuder-Richardson "Formula 20"** (or frequently **KR$_{20}$**) is popular. Which criterion of reliability would the KR$_{20}$ measure? _____ _____

Internal Consistency

339. If items are scored 0 or 1 and we assume the items are equally difficult, an even further simplification in Chronbach's alpha is called the **Kuder-Richardson "Formula 21"** or **KR$_{21}$**. Which of these measures of reliability does not give a measure of the correlation between every item and every other item? Split-half, Chronbach's alpha, KR$_{20}$, Kr$_{21}$.

_____

Which are only appropriate if items are scored 0 and 1? _____ and

_____

Split-Half
KR$_{20}$ and KR$_{21}$

340. Test retest is a measure of _____.

Stability

Validity

341. **Validity** is expressed as the extent to which a test measures what it is supposed to measure (i.e., how well it hits the target). We do not ask whether a test is valid, but for what purpose it is _____.

Valid

342. We will consider four types of validity: predictive, concurrent, construct, and content. Each of these types of validity indicates the test's usefulness for some particular purpose. If we want to know how useful a test is, we have to know how _____ it is for some particular purpose.

Valid

343. Concurrent and predictive validity are measured by the correlation between the test results and some measure called a **criterion.** If we devised a questionnaire to determine the amount of ethyl alcohol consumed by a subject in one week, the grams of ethyl alcohol the subject actually consumed would be the _____.

Criterion

344. The measure of how well a test predicts some future measure (such as aa person's future job or school performance) is called **predictive validity.** In predictive validity the performance predicted by the test is the _____ performance.

Criterion (or Future)

345. If a test were designed to predict grade averages for incoming freshmen, the criterion might be the actual grade average obtained at the end of the freshman year. The test's efficiency at this task would be called its _____ _____.

Predictive Validity

346. You might be interested in how well a test measured some current or recent situation. If high scorers on a leadership test are indeed leaders (as simultaneously determined by judges' ratings), that test could be said to have **concurrent** _____.

Validity

347. The only difference between concurrent and predictive validity is time. A test with concurrent validity seeks to estimate present or recent performance, whereas a test with predictive validity seeks to estimate _____ performance.

Future

348. It is easy to understand a third type of validity, **construct validity,** when you understand the psychological term "construct." A construct ties together a series of related observations. For example, a person might laugh a lot, whistle frequently, speak in resonant tones, and move with unusual vitality. These are all physical observations but if we put them together and say that a person is "happy," we have formed a construct. Similarly, schizophrenia, generosity, goodness, objectivity, maturity, and many other qualities are not simple acts but are _____ derived from a whole set of simple acts.

Constructs

349. Since a construct supposedly links several separate phenomena, these phenomena should hang together (correlate with each other).

According to the *Diagnostic and Statistical Manual of Mental Disorders* (DSM), Bulimia nervosa is characterized in part by:

1. Recurrent episodes of binge eating.
2. A feeling of lack of control over eating behavior during binge eating.
3. Regular use of self-induced vomiting, laxatives or diuretics, strict dieting or fasting, or vigorous exercise in order to prevent weight gain.

If bulimia nervosa is a valid construct, these symptoms should _____ with each other.

Correlate

350. A psychiatrist proposes a construct called the Delmarv Disorder. It is characterized by obsession with

1. **Del**icious food
2. Captain **Marv**el comic books

Follow-up research shows a .03 (essentially zero) correlation between these two phenomena. Discuss the construct validity of the Delmarv disorder. _____

Construct Validity Is Low or Absent.
The Symptoms Do Not Seem to Hang Together.

351. Let's clarify the difference between concurrent (or the related predictive validity) and construct validity. Concurrent validity (and predictive validity) are based on the correlation between related measures being considered on their own. The correlation between the diagnosis from a questionnaire on Psychoactive Substance Dependence and a clinical diagnosis of Psychoactive Substance Dependence would be an example.

Construct validity is based on the correlation or other evidence of relationship between measurements that in themselves are being considered as part of a larger construct. The relationship between a substance being taken in larger amounts or over a longer period than the person intended and the extent to which important social, occupational, or recreational activities are given up or reduced because of substance abuse (both considered diagnostic symptoms) would support the _____ validity of the construct, Psychoactive Substance Abuse.

Construct

352. If a test that had been designed to predict which students would overcome alcoholism by their senior year correlated very well with subsequent clinical findings, we could say that the test had _____ validity.

Predictive

353. An exam for a course should reflect the **content** of the course. The degree to which an examination tests the content of a course is called _____ validity.

Content

354. If the lectures in a course were mostly on French political history but most exam questions inquired about English economic theory, we could say the examination had low _____ _____.

Content Validity

355. For a test to have high validity, it must first of all be reliable. A test could not be used to predict future performance if the test were not _____.

Reliable

Standard Error of Measurement

356. Because every measurement has some unreliability, you can never be certain that one particular administration of a test, for instance, yields the "true" value or score for that individual. If it is not possible to know the "true" value or score, it is desirable to know how far off we might be. This is possible by the use of the standard error of measurement. Does the standard error of measurement allow us to determine the "true" value or score? _____

No

357. The concept of standard error of measurement assumes that the "true" value or score for an individual would be the mean of an infinite number of times that person took the same test, with the assumption that each time she took the test it was as if she had never taken the test before. We are talking here about _____ person taking _____ test _____ _____ _____ of times. We could list each of one individual's scores and draw a curve to fit this population of her test scores. Let us say she is taking the same IQ test a million times. Her various scores on this test might yield a curve such as that shown in the figure.

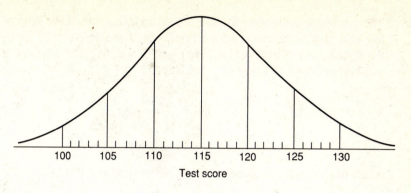

Test score

One   One
An Infinite Number

358. The same percentages apply here as in our standard deviation discussion. Thus 68 percent of this one person's scores on this one test, taken an infinite number of times, would fall within 1σ of her mean score for all the times she took this one test. What percentage of her scores would fall within 2σ of the mean (which we may call her "true" score on the particular test)? _____

---

95 Percent

359. If the mean, 115, is called her "true" score, could she ever get 130 on this same test? _____ Could she ever get 100 on this same test?
_____

Yes
Yes

360. If a person had a Stanford-Binet test score of 120 and the standard error of the test were 5 units, the student might be told that there was a 95 percent chance (you remember this as the area between −2 and +2) that her "true" score was between $120 - (2 * 5) = 110$ and _____.

130

361. This particular administration of the test might be one of the dots at the low end of a distribution about a "true" value or score of 130 (see A in the figure), or it might be at the high end of a distribution about a "true" value or score of 110 (see B in the figure).

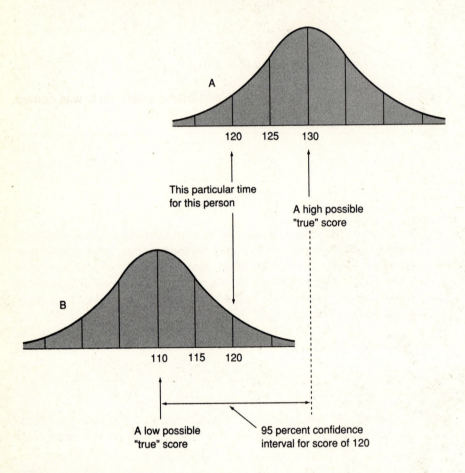

By using the standard error of the mean, do we know the direction in which the true mean lies? _____

No

362. If you know the standard deviation and the reliability coefficient of a test, it is easy to determine its standard error of measurement by the following formula: Standard error of measurement = Standard deviation times the square root of $1 - r$. In the preceding equation, r is the reliability coefficient. What is the standard error of measurement for a test with a standard deviation of 12 and an internal reliability of .75?

$$12 * \sqrt{1 - .75} = 12 * .5 = 6$$

363. The band within which one can feel a certain confidence that a score lies is called a **confidence interval.** The 95 percent confidence interval of the person with the Standard-Binet score of 120 was then _____ to _____. Assuming that this standard error was correct, would it be safe (by safe is meant being wrong a maximum of once out of every 20 or 5 percent of the time) to say that a person with a Stanford-Binet score of 130 was brighter than a person with a Stanford-Binet score of 119? _____

110   130
No

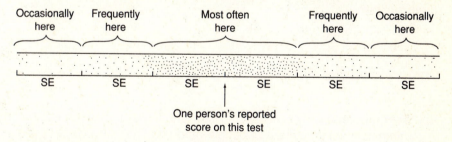

364. When we are presented with some individual measurement, such as an SAT score of 450 or an examination grade of 69, we should not visualize a specific point on a continuum as shown in the figure above. Instead, visualize a hazy band. This hazy band typically extends in either direction from the same position. The true score may be located in a fairly dense area or in a sparse area. Typically, the true score is in a denser area, and you can visualize the following figure with the single reported score occurring in the center. The dots representing possible true scores thin out in areas of limited occurrence at the +3 standard error (SE) positions located on both sides of the reported score.

Occasionally here	Frequently here	Most often here	Frequently here	Occasionally here

| SE | SE | SE | SE | SE | SE |

One person's reported
score on this test

The standard error of measurement lets us set the _____ limits surrounding a given test score. These limits define the space within which a person's "true" score has a given _____ of occurring.

Confidence
Probability

OPEN BOOK QUIZ ON MEASUREMENT
(Answers start on page 187)

1. The correlation between an aptitude test and the achievement that it was being used to predict is a measure of _____.

2. If a test gives very reproducible results, it may be described as _____.

3. If a test has a standard deviation of 10 and a reliability of .64, what is its standard error of measurement? _____

4. If a person gets a score of 550 on a test with a standard error of measurement equal to 15, we could be 95 percent confident that her true score lies between _____ and _____.

5. Which reliability is expressed by the correlation between the score on the same set of items given at two different times? _____

You Can't Fool Me:
Spotting Fallacies in Statistical Thought

This book has introduced statistical methods as powerful tools to illuminate truth and test ideas. There can be a dark side. The use of statistical methods can hide fuzzy thinking. What follows is a review of some common fallacies in statistical thought.

Sampling Problems include **unrepresentative** samples and **inadequate** samples.

Unrepresentative Samples

365. **Testimonials:** Only successful cases tend to be reported. A television infomercial might consist of people reporting their success with some method for making money in real estate. Not heard from are the thousands who lost money. Many reports of medical cures by everything from carrot juice to wearing crystals fall into this category. If, of 200 people who had cancer, we randomly selected 100 who wore crystals inside a box where they couldn't see it and the other 100 wore a similar box but with just a stone for weight, would a comparison of the two groups be a testimonial? _____

No. We're assured of knowing positive and negative outcomes for both the control group and the crystal group.

366. **Casual Samples:** Man-on-the-street interviews taken at 10:00 A.M. would tend to exclude 9-to-5 workers. It would be foolhardy to interpret a survey of subscribers to *Cosmopolitan* as reflecting the views of women in general. A therapist reported that from his observations, gay men were unhappy with their lot. A therapist would tend to see only those who were unhappy. If we wanted to know how the folks in some small town felt about something, would it be accurate if we asked every person present in the town diner? _____

No. This could be a particular section of the population, perhaps people who needed company or who were bad cooks. These speculations might not be true; we just don't know what is.

367. **Extrapolation:** If a little bit is good, a lot would be even better. With no vitamin A, people sicken and die. With perhaps 5000 I.U. of vitamin A, people will do quite well. To extrapolate, one could say, "If 5000 I.U. is good, think how healthy we would be with 500,000 I.U." A dose this size might be fatal.

If we can prove that one hour of exercise a day will cut your chance of a heart attack in half, does it follow that two hours of exercise a day would cut your chances of a heart attack to one quarter? _____

No. Above one hour we have no idea how the curve behaves.

368. **A Fortiori:** If she did this well with no college, think how well she would have done if she had been able to go to college. In the a fortiori fallacy (which translates as "from the strong") we assume that if a person is high in some characteristic, then more of what we think is good would make that person even higher. In the example given, college might actually have decreased the productivity of the woman in question.

If we say of a self-made millionaire: "She would probably have been a billionaire if she had just inherited some money," we are falling into what fallacy? _____ _____

369. **Overgeneralization:** When a sentence begins with "Students today, blacks, Hispanics, men, women, etc.", there is an implication of "all" before the noun. Whatever follows is almost certain to be untrue for many people in that group. When you hear "no, never, always, every, all, etc.," or one of these is implied, beware.

Critique the sentence "In my day we believed in earning our money by an honest day's work." _____

It overgeneralizes.
"We" has the implication of "we all." If that had been
true, there would have been no criminals at that time.
It also has the implication that *today* (compared to "my
day") people *don't* believe in earning money by an honest
day's work, which is also an overgeneralization.

Appendix A

Tables of Critical Values

Table A   Critical Values of the Correlation Coefficient

Table B   The 5 Percent Points for the Distribution of F

Table C   The I Percent Points for the Distribution of F

Table D   Distribution of t Probability

Table E   Distribution of Chi-Square

Table F   Areas and Ordinates of the Normal Curve in Terms of z

A   Critical Values of the Correlation Coefficient

Note: For directions on the use of this table, see pages 79–81.

| df | Level of Significance | | | |
	.10	.05	.02	.01
1	.9877	.9969	.9995	.9999
2	.9000	.9500	.9800	.9900
3	.8054	.8783	.9343	.9587
4	.7293	.8114	.8822	.9172
5	.6694	.7545	.8329	.8745
6	.6215	.7067	.7887	.8343
7	.5822	.6664	.7498	.7977
8	.5494	.6319	.7155	.7646
9	.5214	.6021	.6851	.7348
10	.4973	.5760	.6581	.7079
11	.4762	.5529	.6339	.6835
12	.4575	.5324	.6120	.6614
13	.4409	.5139	.5923	.6411
14	.4259	.4973	.5742	.6226
15	.4124	.4821	.5577	.6055
16	.4000	.4683	.5425	.5897
17	.3887	.4555	.5285	.5751
18	.3783	.4438	.5155	.5614
19	.3687	.4329	.5034	.5487
20	.3598	.4227	.4921	.5368
25	.3233	.3809	.4451	.4869
30	.2960	.3494	.4093	.4487
35	.2746	.3246	.3810	.4182
40	.2573	.3044	.3578	.3932
45	.2428	.2875	.3384	.3721
50	.2306	.2732	.3218	.3541
60	.2108	.2500	.2948	.3248
70	.1954	.2319	.2737	.3017
80	.1829	.2172	.2565	.2830
90	.1726	.2050	.2422	.2673
100	.1638	.1946	.2301	.2540

Abridged from Table VI of Fisher and Yates: "Statistical Tables for Biological, Agricultural and Medical Research," published by Oliver and Boyd Ltd., Edinburgh, and by permission of the authors and publishers.

B   The 5 Percent Points for the Distribution of F

Note: For directions on the use of this table, see pages 116–117.

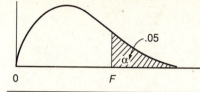

Numerator df

Denom- inator df	1	2	3	4	5	6	8	12	24	∞
1	161.4	199.5	215.7	224.6	230.2	234.0	238.9	243.9	249.0	254.3
2	18.51	19.00	19.16	19.25	19.30	19.33	19.37	19.41	19.45	19.50
3	10.13	9.55	9.28	9.12	9.01	8.94	8.84	8.74	8.64	8.53
4	7.71	6.94	6.59	6.39	6.26	6.16	6.04	5.91	5.77	5.63
5	6.61	5.79	5.41	5.19	5.05	4.95	4.82	4.68	4.53	4.36
6	5.99	5.14	4.76	4.53	4.39	4.28	4.15	4.00	3.84	3.67
7	5.59	4.74	4.35	4.12	3.97	3.87	3.73	3.57	3.41	3.23
8	5.32	4.46	4.07	3.84	3.69	3.58	3.44	3.28	3.12	2.93
9	5.12	4.26	3.86	3.63	3.48	3.37	3.23	3.07	2.90	2.71
10	4.96	4.10	3.71	3.48	3.33	3.22	3.07	2.91	2.74	2.54
11	4.84	3.98	3.59	3.36	3.20	3.09	2.95	2.79	2.61	2.40
12	4.75	3.88	3.49	3.26	3.11	3.00	2.85	2.69	2.50	2.30
13	4.67	3.80	3.41	3.18	3.02	2.92	2.77	2.60	2.42	2.21
14	4.60	3.74	3.34	3.11	2.96	2.85	2.70	2.53	2.35	2.13
15	4.54	3.68	3.29	3.06	2.90	2.79	2.64	2.48	2.29	2.07
16	4.49	3.63	3.24	3.01	2.85	2.74	2.59	2.42	2.24	2.01
17	4.45	3.59	3.20	2.96	2.81	2.70	2.55	2.38	2.19	1.96
18	4.41	3.55	3.16	2.93	2.77	2.66	2.51	2.34	2.15	1.92
19	4.38	3.52	3.13	2.90	2.74	2.63	2.48	2.31	2.11	1.88
20	4.35	3.49	3.10	2.87	2.71	2.60	2.45	2.28	2.08	1.84
21	4.32	3.47	3.07	2.84	2.68	2.57	2.42	2.25	2.05	1.81
22	4.30	3.44	3.05	2.82	2.66	2.55	2.40	2.23	2.03	1.78
23	4.28	3.42	3.03	2.80	2.64	2.53	2.38	2.20	2.00	1.76
24	4.26	3.40	3.01	2.78	2.62	2.51	2.36	2.18	1.98	1.73
25	4.24	3.38	2.99	2.76	2.60	2.49	2.34	2.16	1.96	1.71
26	4.22	3.37	2.98	2.74	2.59	2.47	2.32	2.15	1.95	1.69
27	4.21	3.35	2.96	2.73	2.57	2.46	2.30	2.13	1.93	1.67
28	4.20	3.34	2.95	2.71	2.56	2.44	2.29	2.12	1.91	1.65
29	4.18	3.33	2.93	2.70	2.54	2.43	2.28	2.10	1.90	1.64
30	4.17	3.32	2.92	2.69	2.53	2.42	2.27	2.09	1.89	1.62
40	4.08	3.23	2.84	2.61	2.45	2.34	2.18	2.00	1.79	1.51
60	4.00	3.15	2.76	2.52	2.37	2.25	2.10	1.92	1.70	1.39
120	3.92	3.07	2.68	2.45	2.29	2.17	2.02	1.83	1.61	1.25
∞	3.84	2.99	2.60	2.37	2.21	2.10	1.94	1.75	1.52	1.00

Note: In using this table, the greater mean square must be the numerator of F.

Abridged from Table V of Fisher and Yates: "Statistical Tables for Biological, Agricultural and Medical Research," published by Oliver and Boyd Ltd., Edinburgh, and by permission of the authors and publishers.

C   The 1 Percent Points for the Distribution of F

Note: For directions on the use of this table, see pages 116–117.

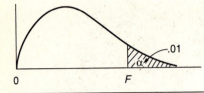

Numerator df

Denom-inator df	1	2	3	4	5	6	8	12	24	∞
1	4052	4999	5403	5625	5764	5859	5982	6106	6234	6366
2	98.50	99.00	99.17	99.25	99.30	99.33	99.37	99.42	99.46	99.50
3	34.12	30.82	29.46	28.71	28.24	27.91	27.49	27.05	26.60	26.12
4	21.20	18.00	16.69	15.98	15.52	15.21	14.80	14.37	13.93	13.46
5	16.26	13.27	12.06	11.39	10.97	10.67	10.29	9.89	9.47	9.02
6	13.74	10.92	9.78	9.15	8.75	8.47	8.10	7.72	7.31	6.88
7	12.25	9.55	8.45	7.85	7.46	7.19	6.84	6.47	6.07	5.65
8	11.26	8.65	7.59	7.01	6.63	6.37	6.03	5.67	5.28	4.86
9	10.56	8.02	6.99	6.42	6.06	5.80	5.47	5.11	4.73	4.31
10	10.04	7.56	6.55	5.99	5.64	5.39	5.06	4.71	4.33	3.91
11	9.65	7.20	6.22	5.67	5.32	5.07	4.74	4.40	4.02	3.60
12	9.33	6.93	5.95	5.41	5.06	4.82	4.50	4.16	3.78	3.36
13	9.07	6.70	5.74	5.20	4.86	4.62	4.30	3.96	3.59	3.16
14	8.86	6.51	5.56	5.03	4.69	4.46	4.14	3.80	3.43	3.00
15	8.68	6.36	5.42	4.89	4.56	4.32	4.00	3.67	3.29	2.87
16	8.53	6.23	5.29	4.77	4.44	4.20	3.89	3.55	3.18	2.75
17	8.40	6.11	5.18	4.67	4.34	4.10	3.79	3.45	3.08	2.65
18	8.28	6.01	5.09	4.58	4.25	4.01	3.71	3.37	3.00	2.57
19	8.18	5.93	5.01	4.50	4.17	3.94	3.63	3.30	2.92	2.49
20	8.10	5.85	4.94	4.43	4.10	3.87	3.56	3.23	2.86	2.42
21	8.02	5.78	4.87	4.37	4.04	3.81	3.51	3.17	2.80	2.36
22	7.94	5.72	4.82	4.31	3.99	3.76	3.45	3.12	2.75	2.31
23	7.88	5.66	4.76	4.26	3.94	3.71	3.41	3.07	2.70	2.26
24	7.82	5.61	4.72	4.22	3.90	3.67	3.36	3.03	2.66	2.21
25	7.77	5.57	4.68	4.18	3.86	3.63	3.32	2.99	2.62	2.17
26	7.72	5.53	4.64	4.14	3.82	3.59	3.29	2.96	2.58	2.13
27	7.68	5.49	4.60	4.11	3.78	3.56	3.26	2.93	2.55	2.10
28	7.64	5.45	4.57	4.07	3.75	3.53	3.23	2.90	2.52	2.06
29	7.60	5.42	4.54	4.04	3.73	3.50	3.20	2.87	2.49	2.03
30	7.56	5.39	4.51	4.02	3.70	3.47	3.17	2.84	2.47	2.01
40	7.31	5.18	4.31	3.83	3.51	3.29	2.99	2.66	2.29	1.80
60	7.08	4.98	4.13	3.65	3.34	3.12	2.82	2.50	2.12	1.60
120	6.85	4.79	3.95	3.48	3.17	2.96	2.66	2.34	1.95	1.38
∞	6.64	4.60	3.78	3.32	3.02	2.80	2.51	2.18	1.79	1.00

Note: In using this table, the greater mean square must be the numerator of F.

Abridged from Table V of Fisher and Yates: "Statistical Tables for Biological, Agricultural and Medical Research," published by Oliver and Boyd Ltd., Edinburgh, and by permission of the authors and publishers.

D Distribution of *t* Probability

Note: For directions on the use of this table, see pages 124–125.

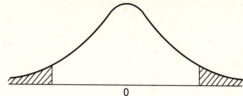

df	P	.10	.05	.01	.001
1		6.314	12.706	63.657	636.619
2		2.920	4.303	9.925	31.598
3		2.353	3.182	5.841	12.941
4		2.132	2.776	4.604	8.610
5		2.015	2.571	4.032	6.859
6		1.943	2.447	3.707	5.959
7		1.895	2.365	3.499	5.405
8		1.860	2.306	3.355	5.041
9		1.833	2.262	3.250	4.781
10		1.812	2.228	3.169	4.587
11		1.796	2.201	3.106	4.437
12		1.782	2.179	3.055	4.318
13		1.771	2.160	3.012	4.221
14		1.761	2.145	2.977	4.140
15		1.753	2.131	2.947	4.073
16		1.746	2.120	2.921	4.015
17		1.740	2.110	2.898	3.965
18		1.734	2.101	2.878	3.922
19		1.729	2.093	2.861	3.883
20		1.725	2.086	2.845	3.850
21		1.721	2.080	2.831	3.819
22		1.717	2.074	2.819	3.792
23		1.714	2.069	2.807	3.767
24		1.711	2.064	2.797	3.745
25		1.708	2.060	2.787	3.725
26		1.706	2.056	2.779	3.707
27		1.703	2.052	2.771	3.690
28		1.701	2.048	2.763	3.674
29		1.699	2.045	2.756	3.659
30		1.697	2.042	2.750	3.646
40		1.684	2.021	2.704	3.551
60		1.671	2.000	2.660	3.460
120		1.658	1.980	2.617	3.373
∞		1.645	1.960	2.576	3.291

Abridged from Table III of R. A. Fisher and F. Yates: "Statistical Tables for Biological, Agricultural, and Medical Research," published by Oliver and Boyd Ltd., Edinburgh. Abridged with permission of the authors and publisher.

E Distribution of Chi-Square

Note: *For directions on the use of this table, see pages 124–125, 130–131.*

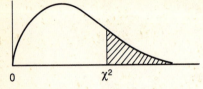

0   χ^2

df	P				
	.10	.05	.02	.01	.001
1	2.706	3.841	5.412	6.635	10.827
2	4.605	5.991	7.824	9.210	13.815
3	6.251	7.815	9.837	11.345	16.266
4	7.779	9.488	11.668	13.277	18.467
5	9.236	11.070	13.388	15.086	20.515
6	10.645	12.592	15.033	16.812	22.457
7	12.017	14.067	16.622	18.475	24.322
8	13.362	15.507	18.168	20.090	26.125
9	14.684	16.919	19.679	21.666	27.877
10	15.987	18.307	21.161	23.209	29.588
11	17.275	19.675	22.618	24.725	31.264
12	18.549	21.026	24.054	26.217	32.909
13	19.812	22.362	25.472	27.688	34.528
14	21.064	23.685	26.873	29.141	36.123
15	22.307	34.996	28.259	30.578	37.697
16	23.542	26.296	29.633	32.000	39.252
17	24.769	27.587	30.995	33.409	40.790
18	25.989	28.869	32.346	34.805	42.312
19	27.204	30.144	33.687	36.191	43.820
20	28.412	31.410	35.020	37.566	45.315
21	29.615	32.671	36.343	38.932	46.797
22	30.813	33.924	37.659	40.289	48.268
23	32.007	35.172	38.968	41.638	49.728
24	33.196	36.415	40.270	42.980	51.179
25	34.382	37.652	41.566	44.314	52.620
26	35.563	38.885	42.856	45.642	54.052
27	36.741	40.113	44.140	46.963	55.476
28	37.916	41.337	45.419	48.278	56.893
29	39.087	42.557	46.693	49.588	58.302
30	40.256	43.773	47.692	50.892	59.703

Abridged from Table IV of Fisher and Yates: "Statistical Tables for Biological, Agricultural and Medical Research," published by Oliver and Boyd Ltd., Edinburgh, and by permission of the authors and publishers.

F   Areas and Ordinates of the Normal Curve in Terms of z

Note: For directions on the use of this table, see pages 32–33.

(1) z Standard Score $\left(\frac{x}{\sigma}\right)$	(2) A Area from Mean to z	(3) B Area in Larger Portion	(4) C Area in Smaller Portion	(5) y Ordinate at z
0.00	.0000	.5000	.5000	.3989
0.01	.0040	.5040	.4960	.3989
0.02	.0080	.5080	.4920	.3989
0.03	.0120	.5120	.4880	.3988
0.04	.0160	.5160	.4840	.3986
0.05	.0199	.5199	.4801	.3984
0.06	.0239	.5239	.4761	.3982
0.07	.0279	.5279	.4721	.3980
0.08	.0319	.5319	.4681	.3977
0.09	.0359	.5359	.4641	.3973
0.10	.0398	.5398	.4602	.3970
0.11	.0438	.5438	.4562	.3965
0.12	.0478	.5478	.4522	.3961
0.13	.0517	.5517	.4483	.3956
0.14	.0557	.5557	.4443	.3951
0.15	.0596	.5596	.4404	.3945
0.16	.0636	.5636	.4364	.3939
0.17	.0675	.5675	.4325	.3932
0.18	.0714	.5714	.4286	.3925
0.19	.0753	.5753	.4247	.3918
0.20	.0793	.5793	.4207	.3910
0.21	.0832	.5832	.4168	.3902
0.22	.0871	.5871	.4129	.3894
0.23	.0910	.5910	.4090	.3885
0.24	.0948	.5948	.4052	.3876
0.25	.0987	.5987	.4013	.3867
0.26	.1026	.6026	.3974	.3857
0.27	.1064	.6064	.3936	.3847
0.28	.1103	.6103	.3897	.3836
0.29	.1141	.6141	.3859	.3825
0.30	.1179	.6179	.3821	.3814
0.31	.1217	.6217	.3783	.3802
0.32	.1255	.6255	.3745	.3790

From *Statistical Methods for the Behavioral Sciences* by Allen L. Edwards. Copyrighted 1954, by Allen L. Edwards. Reprinted by permission of Holt, Rinehart and Winston, Publishers.

F   *(cont.)*

(1) z Standard Score $\left(\dfrac{x}{\sigma}\right)$	(2) A Area from Mean to z	(3) B Area in Larger Portion	(4) C Area in Smaller Portion	(5) y Ordinate at z
0.33	.1293	.6293	.3707	.3778
0.34	.1331	.6331	.3669	.3765
0.35	.1368	.6368	.3632	.3752
0.36	.1406	.6406	.3594	.3739
0.37	.1443	.6443	.3557	.3725
0.38	.1480	.6480	.3520	.3712
0.39	.1517	.6517	.3483	.3697
0.40	.1554	.6554	.3446	.3683
0.41	.1591	.6591	.3409	.3668
0.42	.1628	.6628	.3372	.3653
0.43	.1664	.6664	.3336	.3637
0.44	.1700	.6700	.3300	.3621
0.45	.1736	.6736	.3264	.3605
0.46	.1772	.6772	.3228	.3589
0.47	.1808	.6808	.3192	.3572
0.48	.1844	.6844	.3156	.3555
0.49	.1879	.6879	.3121	.3538
0.50	.1915	.6915	.3085	.3521
0.51	.1950	.6950	.3050	.3503
0.52	.1985	.6985	.3015	.3485
0.53	.2019	.7019	.2981	.3467
0.54	.2054	.7054	.2946	.3448
0.55	.2088	.7088	.2912	.3429
0.56	.2123	.7123	.2877	.3410
0.57	.2157	.7157	.2843	.3391
0.58	.2190	.7190	.2810	.3372
0.59	.2224	.7224	.2776	.3352
0.60	.2257	.7257	.2743	.3332
0.61	.2291	.7291	.2709	.3312
0.62	.2324	.7324	.2676	.3292
0.63	.2357	.7357	.2643	.3271
0.64	.2389	.7389	.2611	.3251
0.65	.2422	.7422	.2578	.3230
0.66	.2454	.7454	.2546	.3209
0.67	.2486	.7486	.2514	.3187
0.68	.2517	.7517	.2483	.3166
0.69	.2549	.7549	.2451	.3144

0.70	.2580	.7580	.2420	.3123
0.71	.2611	.7611	.2389	.3101
0.72	.2642	.7642	.2358	.3079
0.73	.2673	.7673	.2327	.3056
0.74	.2704	.7704	.2296	.3034
0.75	.2734	.7734	.2266	.3011
0.76	.2764	.7764	.2236	.2989
0.77	.2794	.7794	.2206	.2966
0.78	.2823	.7823	.2177	.2943
0.79	.2852	.7852	.2148	.2920
0.80	.2881	.7881	.2119	.2897
0.81	.2910	.7910	.2090	.2874
0.82	.2939	.7939	.2061	.2850
0.83	.2967	.7967	.2033	.2827
0.84	.2995	.7995	.2005	.2803
0.85	.3023	.8023	.1977	.2780
0.86	.3051	.8051	.1949	.2756
0.87	.3078	.8078	.1922	.2732
0.88	.3106	.8106	.1894	.2709
0.89	.3133	.8133	.1867	.2685
0.90	.3159	.8159	.1841	.2661
0.91	.3186	.8186	.1814	.2637
0.92	.3212	.8212	.1788	.2613
0.93	.3238	.8238	.1762	.2589
0.94	.3264	.8264	.1736	.2565
0.95	.3289	.8289	.1711	.2541
0.96	.3315	.8315	.1685	.2516
0.97	.3340	.8340	.1660	.2492
0.98	.3365	.8365	.1635	.2468
0.99	.3389	.8389	.1611	.2444
1.00	.3413	.8413	.1587	.2420
1.01	.3438	.8438	.1562	.2396
1.02	.3461	.8461	.1539	.2371
1.03	.3485	.8485	.1515	.2347
1.04	.3508	.8508	.1492	.2323
1.05	.3531	.8531	.1469	.2299
1.06	.3554	.8554	.1446	.2275
1.07	.3577	.8577	.1423	.2251
1.08	.3599	.8599	.1401	.2227
1.09	.3621	.8621	.1379	.2203
1.10	.3643	.8643	.1357	.2179
1.11	.3665	.8665	.1335	.2155
1.12	.3686	.8686	.1314	.2131
1.13	.3708	.8708	.1292	.2107
1.14	.3729	.8729	.1271	.2083
1.15	.3749	.8749	.1251	.2059
1.16	.3770	.8770	.1230	.2036
1.17	.3790	.8790	.1210	.2012
1.18	.3810	.8810	.1190	.1989

F   *(cont.)*

(1) z Standard Score $\left(\frac{x}{\sigma}\right)$	(2) A Area from Mean to z	(3) B Area in Larger Portion	(4) C Area in Smaller Portion	(5) y Ordinate at z
1.19	.3830	.8830	.1170	.1965
1.20	.3849	.8849	.1151	.1942
1.21	.3869	.8869	.1131	.1919
1.22	.3888	.8888	.1112	.1895
1.23	.3907	.8907	.1093	.1872
1.24	.3925	.8925	.1075	.1849
1.25	.3944	.8944	.1056	.1826
1.26	.3962	.8962	.1038	.1804
1.27	.3980	.8980	.1020	.1781
1.28	.3997	.8997	.1003	.1758
1.29	.4015	.9015	.0985	.1736
1.30	.4032	.9032	.0968	.1714
1.31	.4049	.9049	.0951	.1691
1.32	.4066	.9066	.0934	.1669
1.33	.4082	.9082	.0918	.1647
1.34	.4099	.9099	.0901	.1626
1.35	.4115	.9115	.0885	.1604
1.36	.4131	.9131	.0869	.1582
1.37	.4147	.9147	.0853	.1561
1.38	.4162	.9162	.0838	.1539
1.39	.4177	.9177	.0823	.1518
1.40	.4192	.9192	.0808	.1497
1.41	.4207	.9207	.0793	.1476
1.42	.4222	.9222	.0778	.1456
1.43	.4236	.9236	.0764	.1435
1.44	.4251	.9251	.0749	.1415
1.45	.4265	.9265	.0735	.1394
1.46	.4279	.9279	.0721	.1374
1.47	.4292	.9292	.0708	.1354
1.48	.4306	.9306	.0694	.1334
1.49	.4319	.9319	.0681	.1315
1.50	.4332	.9332	.0668	.1295
1.51	.4345	.9345	.0655	.1276
1.52	.4357	.9357	.0643	.1257
1.53	.4370	.9370	.0630	.1238
1.54	.4382	.9382	.0618	.1219
1.55	.4394	.9394	.0606	.1200

1.56	.4406	.9406	.0594	.1182
1.57	.4418	.9418	.0582	.1163
1.58	.4429	.9429	.0571	.1145
1.59	.4441	.9441	.0559	.1127
1.60	.4452	.9452	.0548	.1109
1.61	.4463	.9463	.0537	.1092
1.62	.4474	.9474	.0526	.1074
1.63	.4484	.9484	.0516	.1057
1.64	.4495	.9495	.0505	.1040
1.65	.4505	.9505	.0495	.1023
1.66	.4515	.9515	.0485	.1006
1.67	.4525	.9525	.0475	.0989
1.68	.4535	.9535	.0465	.0973
1.69	.4545	.9545	.0455	.0957
1.70	.4554	.9554	.0446	.0940
1.71	.4564	.9564	.0436	.0925
1.72	.4573	.9573	.0427	.0909
1.73	.4582	.9582	.0418	.0893
1.74	.4591	.9591	.0409	.0878
1.75	.4599	.9599	.0401	.0863
1.76	.4608	.9608	.0392	.0848
1.77	.4616	.9616	.0384	.0833
1.78	.4625	.9625	.0375	.0818
1.79	.4633	.9633	.0367	.0804
1.80	.4641	.9641	.0359	.0790
1.81	.4649	.9649	.0351	.0775
1.82	.4656	.9656	.0344	.0761
1.83	.4664	.9664	.0336	.0748
1.84	.4671	.9671	.0329	.0734
1.85	.4648	.9678	.0322	.0721
1.86	.4686	.9686	.0314	.0707
1.87	.4693	.9693	.0307	.0694
1.88	.4699	.9699	.0301	.0681
1.89	.4706	.9706	.0294	.0669
1.90	.4713	.9713	.0287	.0656
1.91	.4719	.9719	.0281	.0644
1.92	.4726	.9726	.0274	.0632
1.93	.4732	.9732	.0268	.0620
1.94	.4738	.9738	.0262	.0608
1.95	.4744	.9744	.0256	.0596
1.96	.4750	.9750	.0250	.0584
1.97	.4756	.9756	.0244	.0573
1.98	.4761	.9761	.0239	.0562
1.99	.4767	.9767	.0233	.0551
2.00	.4772	.9772	.0228	.0540
2.01	.4778	.9778	.0222	.0529
2.02	.4783	.9783	.0217	.0519
2.03	.4788	.9788	.0212	.0508
2.04	.4793	.9793	.0207	.0498

F   (cont.)

(1) z Standard Score $\left(\frac{x}{\sigma}\right)$	(2) A Area from Mean to z	(3) B Area in Larger Portion	(4) C Area in Smaller Portion	(5) y Ordinate at z
2.05	.4798	.9798	.0202	.0488
2.06	.4803	.9803	.0197	.0478
2.07	.4808	.9808	.0192	.0468
2.08	.4812	.9812	.0188	.0459
2.09	.4817	.9817	.0183	.0449
2.10	.4821	.9821	.0179	.0440
2.11	.4826	.9826	.0174	.0431
2.12	.4830	.9830	.0170	.0422
2.13	.4834	.9834	.0166	.0413
2.14	.4838	.9838	.0162	.0404
2.15	.4842	.9842	.0158	.0396
2.16	.4846	.9846	.0154	.0387
2.17	.4850	.9850	.0150	.0379
2.18	.4854	.9854	.0146	.0371
2.19	.4857	.9857	.0143	.0363
2.20	.4861	.9861	.0139	.0355
2.21	.4864	.9864	.0136	.0347
2.22	.4868	.9868	.0132	.0339
2.23	.4871	.9871	.0129	.0332
2.24	.4875	.9875	.0125	.0325
2.25	.4878	.9878	.0122	.0317
2.26	.4881	.9881	.0119	.0310
2.27	.4884	.9884	.0116	.0303
2.28	.4887	.9887	.0113	.0297
2.29	.4890	.9890	.0110	.0290
2.30	.4893	.9893	.0107	.0283
2.31	.4896	.9896	.0104	.0277
2.32	.4898	.9898	.0102	.0270
2.33	.4901	.9901	.0099	.0264
2.34	.4904	.9904	.0096	.0258
2.35	.4906	.9906	.0094	.0252
2.36	.4909	.9909	.0091	.0246
2.37	.4911	.9911	.0089	.0241
2.38	.4913	.9913	.0087	.0235
2.39	.4916	.9916	.0084	.0229
2.40	.4918	.9918	.0082	.0224
2.41	.4920	.9920	.0080	.0219
2.42	.4922	.9922	.0078	.0213

2.43	.4925	.9925	.0075	.0208
2.44	.4927	.9927	.0073	.0203
2.45	.4929	.9929	.0071	.0198
2.46	.4931	.9931	.0069	.0194
2.47	.4932	.9932	.0068	.0189
2.48	.4934	.9934	.0066	.0184
2.49	.4936	.9936	.0064	.0180
2.50	.4938	.9938	.0062	.0175
2.51	.4940	.9940	.0060	.0171
2.52	.4941	.9941	.0059	.0167
2.53	.4943	.9943	.0057	.0163
2.54	.4945	.9945	.0055	.0158
2.55	.4946	.9946	.0054	.0154
2.56	.4948	.9948	.0052	.0151
2.57	.4949	.9949	.0051	.0147
2.58	.4951	.9951	.0049	.0143
2.59	.4952	.9952	.0048	.0139
2.60	.4953	.9953	.0047	.0136
2.61	.4955	.9955	.0045	.0132
2.62	.4956	.9956	.0044	.0129
2.63	.4957	.9957	.0043	.0126
2.64	.4959	.9959	.0041	.0122
2.65	.4960	.9960	.0040	.0119
2.66	.4961	.9961	.0039	.0116
2.67	.4962	.9962	.0038	.0113
2.68	.4963	.9963	.0037	.0110
2.69	.4964	.9964	.0036	.0107
2.70	.4965	.9965	.0035	.0104
2.71	.4966	.9966	.0034	.0101
2.72	.4967	.9967	.0033	.0099
2.73	.4968	.9968	.0032	.0096
2.74	.4969	.9969	.0031	.0093
2.75	.4970	.9970	.0030	.0091
2.76	.4971	.9971	.0029	.0088
2.77	.4972	.9972	.0028	.0086
2.78	.4973	.9973	.0027	.0084
2.79	.4974	.9974	.0026	.0081
2.80	.4974	.9974	.0026	.0079
2.81	.4975	.9975	.0025	.0077
2.82	.4976	.9976	.0024	.0075
2.83	.4977	.9977	.0023	.0073
2.84	.4977	.9977	.0023	.0071
2.85	.4978	.9978	.0022	.0069
2.86	.4979	.9979	.0021	.0067
2.87	.4979	.9979	.0021	.0065
2.88	.4980	.9980	.0020	.0063
2.89	.4981	.9981	.0019	.0061
2.90	.4981	.9981	.0019	.0060
2.91	.4982	.9982	.0018	.0058

F   (cont.)

(1) z Standard Score $\left(\frac{x}{\sigma}\right)$	(2) A Area from Mean to z	(3) B Area in Larger Portion	(4) C Area in Smaller Portion	(5) y Ordinate at z
2.92	.4982	.9982	.0018	.0056
2.93	.4983	.9983	.0017	.0055
2.94	.4984	.9984	.0016	.0053
2.95	.4984	.9984	.0016	.0051
2.96	.4985	.9985	.0015	.0050
2.97	.4985	.9985	.0015	.0048
2.98	.4986	.9986	.0014	.0047
2.99	.4986	.9986	.0014	.0046
3.00	.4987	.9987	.0013	.0044
3.01	.4987	.9987	.0013	.0043
3.02	.4987	.9987	.0013	.0042
3.03	.4988	.9988	.0012	.0040
3.04	.4988	.9988	.0012	.0039
3.05	.4989	.9989	.0011	.0038
3.06	.4989	.9989	.0011	.0037
3.07	.4989	.9989	.0011	.0036
3.08	.4990	.9990	.0010	.0035
3.09	.4990	.9990	.0010	.0034
3.10	.4990	.9990	.0010	.0033
3.11	.4991	.9991	.0009	.0032
3.12	.4991	.9991	.0009	.0031
3.13	.4991	.9991	.0009	.0030
3.14	.4992	.9992	.0008	.0029
3.15	.4992	.9992	.0008	.0028
3.16	.4992	.9992	.0008	.0027
3.17	.4992	.9992	.0008	.0026
3.18	.4993	.9993	.0007	.0025
3.19	.4993	.9993	.0007	.0025
3.20	.4993	.9993	.0007	.0024
3.21	.4993	.9993	.0007	.0023
3.22	.4994	.9994	.0006	.0022
3.23	.4994	.9994	.0006	.0022
3.24	.4994	.9994	.0006	.0021
3.30	.4995	.9995	.0005	.0017
3.40	.4997	.9997	.0003	.0012
3.50	.4998	.9998	.0002	.0009
3.60	.4998	.9998	.0002	.0006
3.70	.4999	.9999	.0001	.0004

Appendix B

Bibliography

For those who might like to forge ahead on their own, there are now many good, clear texts. The following brief personal list omits many fine books and is in the spirit of some suggestions the author would give if someone were to ask, "Where would be a good place to look for more detail on _____?"

Advanced

Hays, William L., *Statistics,* 5th ed. (New York: Harcourt Brace Jovanovich, 1994), is thorough and clear. It contains SAS programs.

Tabachnick, Barbara G., and Linda S. Fidell, *Using Multivariate Statistics,* 2nd ed. (New York: HarperCollins, 1989) is excellent. It uses not only SAS and SPSS but also BMDP and SYSTAT.

Computer Packages

Minitab Reference Manual. Different manuals for the various platforms. These are clear, detailed, and suitable for any level.

Cody, Ronald P., and Jeffrey K. Smith, *Applied Statistics and the SAS Programming Language* 3rd ed. (New York: North-Holland, 1991), is clear and has many exercises with solutions in the back.

SAS/STAT User's Guide, Version 6, 4th ed., vols. 1 and 2, (Cary, N.C.: SAS Institute, 1989), have examples with unnecessarily long datatsets but are very thorough and rather inexpensive.

SPSS has different manuals for various platforms. Examples are: *SPSS Base System Syntax Reference Guide,* Release 6.1 (SPSS Inc.), 1994.

SPSS for Windows Base System Users Guide, Release 6.1 (SPSS), 1994.

Appendix C

Use of Computer Packages: An Overview

The optional sections entitled Computer Quick Start give a fast and gentle introduction to the use of three popular, powerful, and easy-to-use computer packages for data analysis: MINITAB, SAS, and SPSS.

If none of these packages are available, the Computer Quick Start sections may still serve to demonstrate the ease of using packages and how output looks.

All sections use the same data that have been used throughout. The data are in a separate file, here arbitrarily called **demo.dat,** which looks like the following:

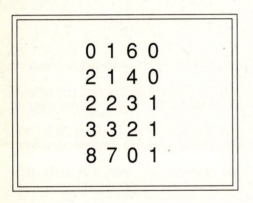

```
0 1 6 0
2 1 4 0
2 2 3 1
3 3 2 1
8 7 0 1
```

The four variables (each column is a variable) are arbitrarily named x, y, z and group. Spaces or commas between columns make it easier to read in external data.

This is a tiny version of the case in which we might have a large file of data and do various analyses on it, sometimes using different procedures, packages, or groups of variables.

With all three packages we will use program files that tell the computer what data to operate on and what to do with it. These have names such as **desc_mtb.pgm** or **desc_sas.pgm, or desc_sps.sps.** The names are arbitrary and designed to make it easy to know how the file is used. The program file named **desc_mtb.pgm** would work just as well if it were named **silly.foo.** As long as names are limited to eight letters or digits before the decimal point and three digits after it, have no spaces, and are unique, almost anything will work.

A sample of a program file for MINITAB called **desc_mtb.pgm** is

```
READ       'demo.dat'        C1 — C4
NAME       C1 'x'   C2   'y'   C3   'z'   C4   'group'
DESC       C1 — C4
```

The **C1— –C4** means from **Column 1 through Column 4.** Names are enclosed in single quotes. To the computer, uppercase or lowercase usually doesn't matter. For clarity to humans, in this book, UPPERCASE will be used where a particular form must be used, and lower case will be used for arbitrary names. DESC is short for DESCRIBE and results in a descriptive analysis of the data.

The corresponding file for SAS, desc_sas.pgm is

```
DATA;
INFILE  'demo.dat';
INPUT   x   y   z   group;
PROC UNIVARIATE;
RUN;
```

The **DATA;** line is for complex data handling. We need only use it as above. **INFILE 'demo.dat';** brings in the external data file, demo.dat, and the **INPUT x y z group;** line reads the data and assigns names. **PROC UNIVARIATE;** commands SAS to do the procedure called UNIVARIATE, which is a descriptive data analysis. **RUN;** tells SAS to run the procedure.

For SPSS, the comparable file, **desc_sps.sps** is:

```
DATA LIST
  FILE= demo.dat
  FREE/ x   y   z   group.
DESC
  VARS= ALL
  /STATS= ALL.
```

DATA LIST starts the data input. The FILE= line gives the name of the file containing the data. FREE/ causes data to be read in free form. Leave a blank at start of all lines except first of a command and notice . at end of command. Abbreviations to three places will generally work. The entire name for the command is DESCRIPTIVES. SPSS requires a VARIABLES statement but will usually accept VARS as sufficient.

Program files in all of the packages read in data, assign names to the variables, and tell the computer what procedures to carry out.

The brief coverage in this book only hints at the power of these packages. They are all capable of sophisticated professional analysis and stunning graphics.

Appendix B has several references that will help you further.

General Instructions for MINITAB

After you start MINITAB by entering **MINITAB** at your particular system prompt, you will get a prompt that looks like **MTB >.** With a program file and data file available in the computer, enter **EXEC 'desc_mtb.pgm'** (Enter) or whatever file name you used. Note the single quote marks around the file name. MINITAB requires them.

A path is a series of names that tell a computer where to find a file in its memory. A typical path might read: **'c:\mtbwin\data\desc_mtb.pgm'.** This tells the computer that the file **desc_mtb.pgm** is in a directory called data that is a subdirectory of the directory **mtbwin,** which is on the **C** drive. If you do need a path, it goes before the file name. Both the path and file name go inside the quotes. The EXEC command might now look like **EXEC 'c:\mtbwin\data\desc_mtb.pgm'**

The **.pgm** ending is used here to make MINITAB and SAS as comparable as possible. If you use **.mtb** as the end of MINITAB program names, as **desc_mtb.mtb,** you won't have to use any ending in an **EXEC** statement. You could enter **EXEC 'desc_mtb'.** Use whichever form you like.

Hard Copy Using Minitab

If you want paper output (hard copy), type **OUTFILE 'desc_mtb.out'** (Enter) **before** you type the EXEC line. A file will be created as the program executes. The location where it is deposited varies by system and your setup, but it would be typical for it to go into a directory called **minitab/data.** When done, type **STOP** and MINITAB will put you back into the system.

The output file can now be edited and printed by using any word processor. Labels that you could not manage to have the MINITAB supply are easily added. One final note on getting paper output: A line **before** the exec line on which you enter **OH = 0** will cause the screen to scroll without stopping when a program executes. This step avoids having the computer ask for confirmation that you would like it to continue. Such dialogue clutters output.

Using SAVE does not give you a file that you can print. It saves the present state of the computer to a file called **MINITAB.MTW** (for **M**INITAB **W**ORK). This file is unreadable by anything except MINITAB, but if you came back months later, started up MINITAB, and typed **RE-TRIEVE** (Enter), all would be as you had left it.

Interactive Minitab

Interactive computing is a popular alternative to the approach of using data files and program files. It is fine for small sets of data and simple programs but awkward for serious work.

This approach can be demonstrated by the following sequence after having logged onto MINITAB:

```
MTB  > SET C1
DATA> 0 2 2 3 8
DATA> END
MTB  > SET C2
DATA> 1 1 2 3 7
DATA> END
MTB  > SET C3
DATA> 6 4 3 2 0
DATA> END
MTB  > SET C4
DATA> 0 0 1 1 1
DATA> END
MTB  > NAME C1 'x' C2 'y' C3 'z' C4 'group'
MTB  > DESC C1— –C4
```

The output is the same as before. This method has the advantage of not involving external files. It has the disadvantage that you must make correct entries each time you use MINITAB and that the data are not as easily used by other packages. With .pgm (or .mtb) files, you can have basic programs for frequently used procedures, change them slightly, and **EXEC**ute the program.

A combination will often be useful. You might EXECute a program file and then decide that there are some other questions you would like to ask of the data. You can enter the commands in interactive mode from that point on. The data are already in and named. Any time you want to be reminded of what data are entered and what columns they are in, type INFO. One parting thought: MINITAB has exceedingly friendly help. Enter **HELP** at **MTB >.**

You will have explanations and examples at your fingertips.

General Instructions for SAS

After you start SAS, you should be in the PROGRAM EDITOR at a **Command** → prompt. If you wish to submit the program file called desc_sas.pgm for execution, you enter **INCLUDE 'desc_sas.pgm'** and the file should appear. If you would like a full-screen display, type **Z** (for ZOOM) at the command line. Still on the command line, you can now enter **SUB** (for SUBMIT) and the file executes. If all has gone well, the progress of the analysis will be reported in the upper right and after a few moments the completed output will appear. This will be in a different window, the OUTPUT window. If you want to print or perhaps edit the output, you can save it to a regular file by typing on the Command line of the OUTPUT WINDOW; **FILE 'desc_sas.out'** or whatever name you would like. SAS will report the number of lines written to a file. If you wish, the file can be edited in your favorite word processor and printed.

When Things Go Wrong

While MINITAB and SAS are both powerful and easy to use,
SAS is more powerful than MINITAB but is also more vulnerable to format and grammar problems. There is a likelihood that an error will occur. In addition, the program will have vanished. Don't fret. Get it back by entering **RECALL** at the **Command** →.

There are three screens to know about for now: the **PGM** screen (PROGRAM EDITOR) where you started, the **OUT** screen where OUTPUT will appear if all goes well, and the LOG screen (which appeared above your PGM screen at the beginning). You can get to any screen from any other screen by typing **PGM, OUT,** or **LOG** as desired at any command line. There are other screens, but these three will get you started. The LOG screen may help you diagnose what went wrong. It holds a record of your attempt to run the program. It is good practice to type **CLEAR** at the command line of the log screen after each use, or you can type **CLEAR LOG** at the **Command** → of any screen. To fix a program, you can use the line editor that is included on the PROGRAM EDITOR screen or ask your local systems person how you can edit the screen with a word processor. However you get the program working, to keep a copy of the working program, enter **PGM** at the **Command** → of any screen, enter **RECALL** to get program back, and enter **FILE 'desc_sas.pgm'** (or whatever file name you used).

If you type **HELP** at the **Command** →, you will enter SAS HELP. Many find this to be a frustrating maze, but it must help some people, and you may be one of them. If you get trapped or are simply ready to leave, go to the command line and enter **END**.

   To exit SAS, enter **BYE** at the **Command** → of any window. **INTER-ACTIVE SAS** is possible but is not recommended. Once you get a file working, save it and then modify it for future runs.

General Instructions for SPSS

Assume that you have a file of SPSS commands. The file could be named **DESC_SPS.PGM** but SPSS reacts more gracefully if the program file has an ending of **SPS** (thus DESC_SPS.SPS).

   Assume that the date file (demo.dat in this example) and the program file (desc_sps.sps in this example) are in the same directory as SPSS. If they are not, you can use a path statement as shown earlier. If you are on a VAX, enter SPSS desc_sps.sps and tap **return**. The analysis will proceed. If you are using SPSS for Windows, click on **File,** then **Open,** then **SPSS syntax.** A window will open showing all the .SPS files that are in the active directory. Double click on the one that you want to run (desc_sps.sps in this case.) The file will appear in a useful editing window. Select the entire file with the mouse, double click **RUN** and the output will appear.

When Things Go Wrong

SPSS has rigid requirements about the input format (syntax). When things go wrong, helpful error messages may be in the output window. If you are on a VAX computer, reedit the .sps file in any available editor (such as EVE.)

   If you are using SPSS for Windows, bring the SPSS syntax (input) window to the front and edit the file. You can easily view the input and output windows at the same time.

   With SPSS, **.lst** is the default ending for output files. The output file would be called **desc_sps.lst** in the present example. You can edit the output as you would edit any file, deleting unwanted output or adding labels or comments that you did not know to create within the program.

Final Thoughts

All three packages have Windows and Macintosh versions with the ease of use these imply. All three have fine documentation with free, helpful, and friendly telephone support when you have problems. The approach to all three packages that was used in this text was to present a few lines for each that work on any platform.

Appendix D

Answers to Open Book Quizzes

Frequency Distribution (page 5–6)

1.
Scores	f
0	I
1	II
2	III
3	II
4	0
5	I

2. and 3.

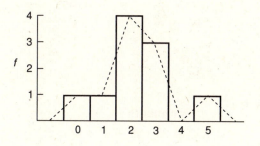

4. Y, X

5. Y
   X

Averages (page 20)

Answers	Comments
1a. 6	
1b. 5.5	Remember to order scores from low to high: 3, 5, 5, 6, 8, 9.
1c. 5	More 5's than anything else.
2. Positively skewed	
3. Median	Extreme score, therefore don't use mean.

The Normal Curve (page 34)

Answers	**Comments**
1. Normal	See Frame 53
2. .05 or 5 percent	$.025 + .025 = 0.5$

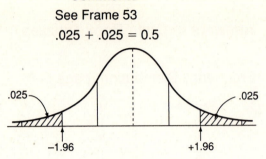

3. .90 or 90 percent

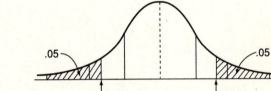

4. Inflection point
5. 68 percent

Variability (page 54)

Answers

1. 16

$(\Sigma X)^2/N = 64$

$SS = 80 - 64 = 16$

2. 2
3. 2

4. 4
5. B

Comments

$\Sigma X^2 = 2^2 + 2^2 + 6^2 + 6^2 = 80$

$SD = SS/N = 16/4 = 2$

Adding a constant (1 in this case) to each score does not change the SD.

$6 - 2$

Scores of A are mostly bunched together.

Probability (page 62)

Answers

1. We reject the H_0.
2. .81
3. .09
4. It will go up.

Comments

$.9 * .9$

$.9 * .1$

5. .001

The alpha (or significance) level is the maximum probability of making a Type I error.

Confidence Intervals (page 71)

Answers	**Comments**
1. .05	$s_{\bar{x}} = s\sqrt{N} = 4.0/\sqrt{64}$ $= 4.0/8.0 = .5$
2. 2.00	$N - 1 = 64 - 1 = 63$ which is not available in the t table, but 60 is very close. If $N - 1$ was much more diverse from any given table value, one could interpolate or, better yet, locate a more complete table.
3. 1.00	$t * s_{\bar{x}} = 2 * .5 = 1.0$ or $t * \text{SEMEAN} = 2 * .5 = 1$
4. 89.0;	Lower boundary $= \text{Mean} - (t * \text{SEMEAN})$ $= 90.0 - 1.0$
91.0	Upper boundary $= \text{Mean} + (t * \text{SEMEAN})$ $= 90.0 + 1.0$
5. .05 or 5 percent	If the probability that the true or actual population mean lies within the confidence interval $= 95\%$, then $100\% - 95\% = 5\%$.

Correlation Coefficient (page 84–85)

Answers	**Comments**
1. Positively correlated	
2. A	
3. Not true	
4. +.5	$\Sigma XY = 13 \; \Sigma X = \Sigma Y = 6$ $N = 3$ $SP = 13 - \dfrac{6 * 6}{3} = 1$ $\Sigma X^2 = \Sigma Y^2 = 14$ $SS = 14 - (6^2/3) = -2$ $r = \dfrac{1}{\sqrt{2 * 2}} = .5$

5. $-.5$

$\Sigma XY = 11$; All else is the same as Question 4.

$$SP = 11 - (6^2/3) = -1$$

$$r = \frac{-1}{\sqrt{2 * 2}} = -1/2 = -.5$$

Regression (page 105–106)

Answers

Comments

1. 1.2

$r = .6$

$$Z_{Y \, pred} = r * z$$
$$= .6 * 2 = 1.2$$

2. .25

$$SP = 20 - \frac{(6 * 9)}{3} = 2$$

$$SS_x = 20 - \frac{6^2}{3} = 8$$

$$b = \frac{SP}{SS_x} = \frac{2}{8} = .25$$

3. 2.5

$$a = \overline{Y} - b\overline{X} = 3 - .25 * 2$$
$$= 3 - .5 = 2.5$$

4. 3.5

$$y_{pred} = a + bX$$
$$= 2.5 + .25(4)$$
$$= 2.5 + 1 = 3.5$$

5. C

The type of regression analysis that we've studied is appropriate only for **linear** (straight-line) relationships.

Analysis of Variance (ANOVA) (page 121–122)

Answers

Comments

1. Mean

2. Within

Between SS + Within SS = Total SS

2a. 4

2b. 8

Source	SS	df	MS	F
Total	20	3		
Between	16	1	15	8
Within	4	2	2	

3. No

18.51 is needed, but we got only 8 (see F Table following Frame 000). Go across to 1 and down to 2.

Chi-Square (Frequencies: Expected and Observed) (page 139)

Answers	Comments
1. Analysis of variance (or ANOVA)	See Frame 230
Chi-square	See Frame 270 and 271
2. Difference is significant	Expected are 10 10 10

$$\chi^2 = \frac{(5 - 10)^2}{10} + \frac{(20 - 10)^2}{10} + \frac{(5 - 10)^2}{10}$$

$$= 2.5 + 10 + 2.5 = 15$$

With 2 df, the critical chi-square value at the .05 level is 5.99, which is beaten by the chi-square of 15.

Answers	Comments
3. 15	$(60 * 30)/120$
4. 15.34	$1.67 + 1.67 + 1 + 1 + 5 + 5$
5. 5.99	df = (Rows − 1) * (Columns − 1)
	= 1 * 2

Measurement (page 158)

Answers	Comments
1. Validity (or predictive validity)	
2. Reliable	
3. 6	
4. 520 and 580	$550 + (2 * 15) = 580$
5. Test-retest	See Frame 323

Appendix E

Evaluative Data

The quality of programmed instruction depends strongly on feedback cycles; the author creates some material and tries it out on students. The tryout reveals sections that teach particularly efficiently, sections so repetitive that they are dull, and sections so dense that they baffle. The cycle closes as the author, using the results of criterion testing, completed programs, interviews with students, and questions raised during class, prepares a new version that should correct earlier problems but almost invariably introduces some new (usually fewer) difficulties, and distributes this new material for yet another try. Repeated cycling with diverse students is an ongoing process, resulting in material that, while always short of perfection, gets constantly better.

Sites used in feedback cycles up to now include those shown in the table. In addition to these specific studies, many helpful suggestions and criticisms have been received from students and teachers during the 30 years since the first edition of *Statistical Concepts: A Basic Program* was published. This frequently detailed and insightful informal feedback has led to significant improvements in this third edition.

Level	Course	School
Undergrad and Grad	Intro Stat (for 30 successive years) Experimental Psych	State University College at Oneonta, Oneonta, New York
Undergrad and Grad Nurses	Intro Stat with medical emphasis	A.O. Fox Memorial Hospital, Oneonta, New York
Undergrad	Educational Psychology	Brigham Young University, Provo, Utah
Undergrad	Educational Psychology	University of Toledo, Toledo, Ohio
Undergrad Graduate	Intro Psych Guidance	Cornell University, Ithaca, New York
Undergrad	Intro Stat and Educational Measurement	Jackson State College, Jackson, Mississippi
High School	Special	Four Upper New York State Counties
Seventh Grade	Special	Bugbee School, Oneonta, New York

Index

Additive law 60, 136, 138
Alpha error.. 57
Analysis of variance (ANOVA) 106
      using MINITAB 119
      using SAS 120
      using SPSS 121
Answers to open book quizzes 183
Asymmetrical 10
Averages 6

Beta error 56
Between subjects design 113
Between variance 111
Biased sample 47
Bimodal distribution 17

Central tendency 6
Chi-square 123-126, 130, 131
Chronbach's alpha 149
College Board (CEEB) scores (SAT) 35
Confidence interval 56, 68, 157
Construct validity 152
Correction factor (CF) 43
Correlation using SAS 82
Correlation coefficient 72, 73, 78, 148
Correlation coefficient: practical computations 76
      using MINITAB 82
      using SAS 82
      using SPSS 83, 104

Degrees of freedom (df) 66, 67, 124
Descriptive statistics 45
Distribution 1

Equivalent forms reliability 148
Evaluative data 188

F ratio 109-111
Fallacies 158
Formula for r 77
Frequency 1, 20
Frequency distribution 1
Frequency polygon 2

General instructions
    for MINITAB 178
    for SAS 180
    for SPSS 181
General regression formula 92

Histogram 2

Inferential statistics 45
Internal consistency 148

Laws of probability 59
Levels of significance 110
Line of best fit 93
Linear regression 99

Marginals 128
Mean 6, 35
Mean square 115
Mean square between groups 108
Mean square (MS) 108
Mean: practical computations 7
Measurement 59, 140
Median 6, 13
Mode 6, 15-17
Multimodal 17
Multiplicative law 60

Negative correlation 72
Normal (bell) curve 20, 22
Normalized regression coefficient 92
Null hypothesis 55, 56, 59, 108, 117, 128, 131

Observed frequency (O) 127

Parameter 48
Percentage score 140
Percentile rank (PR) 143
Point estimation 48
Points of inflection 24
Population 46
Positive correlation 72
Predicting behavior: computations 101
Prediction 85
Predictive validity 151
Probability 55, 58
Product moment correlation coefficient 73

Range 38, 49
Rank 141
Raw score 140
Regression 81, 91
Regression coefficient 90
    using MINITAB 102
    using SAS 103
Reliability and validity 146
Reliable 154

Sample 46
Sample and population 46
SAT Verbal scores 90
Significance of a correlation coefficient 79
Significance tests 48
Significant 58
Simple random sample 47
Skewed 8
Slope 86
Split-half 148
Square of r 79
Standard deviation 24, 26, 35, 39-41, 48
Standard error of the mean 64
Standard error of measurement 156
Standard of measurement 154
Standard score 35, 145
Stanford-Binet IQ scores 36
Statistic 48
Subjects 106
Sum of squares (SS) 40, 41
Symbol for estimate of population standard deviation 51
Symbol for population standard deviation 50
Symmetrical 10, 91

t test 118
Test-retest reliability 148
Tied-scores rank 145
Type I error 57
Type II error 57

Use of computer packages: an overview 176

Validity: predictive, concurrent, construct, content 150
Variability 38
Variables 1
Variance 51

Wechsler IQ scores 36
Within groups 107
Within subjects design 113

Y_{pred} 87

Z score 27, 28, 31, 90